Published by
EN Productions
P.O. Box 1653, Franklin, TN 37065
Office Phone: 615-599-5552
Office Fax: 615-599-5554
For orders call: 1-877-200-1604
www.encountersnetwork.com

GET eSchool and Other Materials

The following *Consecrated Contemplative Prayer* study guide is great for individual study in your own home, with a small group, or in a classroom setting. It also serves as part of the core curriculum for a course by the same title in our God Encounters Training – eSchool of the Heart (visit www.GETeSchool.com for more info). At the end of each detailed lesson are simple questions for your reflection and review. In a back section of this study guide, you will find the answers to these questions to aid in your learning.

If you have benefited from this study guide, James W. Goll has many other study guides and materials available for purchase. You may place orders for materials from Encounters Network's Resource Center on our website at www.encountersnetwork.com or by calling 1-877-200-1604. You may also mail your orders to P.O. Box 470470, Tulsa, OK, 74147-0470. For more information, visit our website or send an e-mail to info@encountersnetwork.com.

Dedication and Acknowledgement

This set of teachings has come forth from the gleanings of various pastors, teachers, and authors. In recent years, there has been an explosion of new books and literature on various subjects of prayer. But, as of yet, there are few contemporary writings on this theme of contemplation.

I wish to express thanks to our Lord for the writings of Richard J. Foster. His books, *Prayer: Finding the Heart's True Home*, and, *Devotional Classics* are modern day gems that show forth a reflection of the Holy Spirit's presence through the spiritual disciplines of quietness. Mark and Patti Virkler's book, *Communion with God*, has been a light in the midst of darkness to me as well.

But I wish to dedicate this study guide to my dear friend, Pat Gastineau, of Roswell, Georgia. Many talk about the Interior Castle, but few actually let the love of God penetrate their hidden rooms. Thank you, Pat, for helping to guide me into a deeper union with Christ. Bless you, Steve Meeks, Senior Pastor of Calvary Community Church in Houston, Texas. You are indeed a forerunner and your teaching and practices are a beautiful model. Thank you, the late wonderful Bob Lyon, my missionary friend of many years, Marcus Young, and others. Thanks for reflecting His light.

Dr. James W. Goll
Encounters Network

Table of Contents

Preface: A Contemplative Lifestyle

Have you ever read Psalm 23? No, I mean really read it slowly and let the meaning of it sink into the very core of your being? Let's see – how does it go? Oh yes, *The Lord is my shepherd, I shall not want. He makes me to...*

I think we need to start out all over again! In fact, if you will give me some grace I am even going to add in an opening qualifying word. Here we go - now read this slowly! When the Lord is my shepherd, I shall not want. He makes me to lie down in the green pastures. He leads me beside the quiet stream. There He restores my soul.

Oh, I can feel it right now as I pen this to you. Yes, when the Lord is my shepherd, He will lead me to the quiet stream. Yes, it is true, that is the place where He restores my soul – the quiet stream! Oh, how we need this return to a 'quietist movement' in our generation! We need to learn the lost art of quieting our soul before the Lord in order to come into greater union with our Messiah. We need a wordless baptism to be immersed in!

Want to hear a descriptive definition of what it means to walk in the Spirit? To walk in the Spirit is to walk so closely with Jesus so as to only cast one shadow! Does your heart long for this? Do you long to cast just one shadow and it not be your own? That is the lifestyle of those who reflect upon the beauty of the Lord and bask in His radiant presence. Yes, worshipping, waiting, listening, longing and yearning for His presence is the lifestyle of the contemplative Christian. It's for you and it's for me!

That is what this study guide, *Consecrated Contemplative Prayer*, is all about! It was designed with you in mind. If you want to go deeper in your life of communion with the lover of your soul, then get ready, for these materials were forged in the fiery furnace of God's majestic love as a tool to help you grow in intimacy with Christ Jesus, our great Lord!

This study guide is broken down into twelve lessons with Reflection Questions at the end of each lesson and an answer key at the back of the manual. This guide has three sections. The first one is devoted to the subject of **Quieting Our Souls before God**. Vintage material is found here.

The second section is simply titled **Contemplative Prayer**. Here I teach you what contemplative prayer is and what it is not. We continue with great lessons on "The Center of Quiet" and the "Journey into the Interior Castle". Once again, I take you on a journey less traveled, but one that your heart and soul will find delightful.

The third and final section is new material I have prepared on **Cultivating Spiritual Disciplines**. Here we glance at "Christian Meditative Prayer," "The Fasted Life," "Towards a Greater Union," and "Walking through the Tabernacle." Great lessons with wonderful insights ready for you to devour as your next meal!

I trust that you will be as blessed in working through this study guide as I have been fulfilled in preparing it! Take and eat, for this is the diet for all who would take up the lifestyle of the contemplative - a life wasted on God!

Blessings to You!

James W. Goll

Section One:

Quieting Our Souls before God

Lesson One:
The Inward for the Outward

I. SCRIPTURES ON "INWARDNESS"

A. Isaiah 30:15
In quietness and confidence shall be your strength.

B. John 14:20
And in that day you shall know that I am in the Father, and you in Me, and I in you.

C. I Cor. 3:16
Do you not know that you are a temple of God and that the Spirit of God dwells <u>in</u> you?

D. I Cor. 6:17, 19
But the one who joins himself to the Lord is one spirit with Him...Or do you not know that your body is a Temple of the Holy Spirit who <u>is in you</u>, whom you have from God, and that you are not your own.

E. Col. 1:26, 27
That is, the mystery which has been hidden from the past ages and generations, but has now been manifested to His saints, to whom God willed to make know what is the riches of the glory of this mystery, which is CHRIST IN YOU THE HOPE OF GLORY.

II. NEW CREATION REALITIES – THE SHADOW FULFILLED

A. Old Testament Tabernacle of Moses
The Old Testament tabernacle of Moses was a shadow of New Testament realities, even as it had three compartments. As it had the Outer Court, the Inner Court and the Holy of Holies, so also are we made of spirit, soul, and body. In the very center of the Holy of Holies was the Ark of the Covenant containing the law, Aaron's rod that budded, and the manna from the wilderness. Then on top lay the covering cherubim and the mercy seat of God. God dwells in our heart (the Most Holy Place) by faith in Christ Jesus. Therefore, we find that the shadow of the Old Testament fulfilled by the New Creation of Christ dwelling in our hearts through faith.

11

B. Lazarus Word

Let us break the hard, outer shell (husk) off our lives so the tender shoot of God's life from within may arise. We must cooperate with His breaking in order that His life will flourish. Even as Lazarus was raised from the dead and new life came, we also shall spring forth out of hardness into a place of tenderness within. Let His new life spring forth!

III. A VISIONARY EXPERIENCE

I had a visionary encounter where I was shown seven consecutive doorways through which we proceed in order to come into greater union with Christ. I could read these words written over each doorpost in this encounter.

A. Seven Consecutive Doorways

1. The inward journey (an invitation to enter into)
2. Forgiveness (having a clear conscience)
3. Cleansing by the power of the blood
4. Lowliness of heart (the quality of humility)
5. Grace (from the Father towards us)
6. Mercy (towards others through us)
7. Union with Christ (II Cor. 6:17)

B. A Continual Journey

We are each at different stages of growth in our Christian experience. I have just described for you part of my "Revelatory Pilgrimage" into the interior life message that the Lord may lead you. He is a great instructor! But He wants us to grasp more than just knowledge about Him. He wants us to "Know Him." At different seasons in your life you will pass through different doorways; rest assured - it is a continual journey of cleansing, knowing and being known.

IV. FROM THE WRITINGS OF MARTHA WING ROBINSON [1]

Martha Wing Robinson (1874-1936) was a Pentecostal preacher and a leader of Zion Faith Homes in Zion, Illinois. She was known as a carrier of the presence of God as told in the biography *Radiant Glory*.

True Inwardness of a Christian

When Jesus first sets vessels to love Him, He wants them to see Him all the time, every moment, and if they are very much in earnest, to live that way – moment by moment.

In the beginning of such experience, most of the time they pray, praise, wait on God, commune, and often, if at work, see Jesus in the soul.

If they grow in this experience and become vessels of God for His use, they begin to seek more for Him, and He comes more to them, for He does to all who seek Him from the heart.

Also, He begins to draw their thoughts all the time – every moment – to Himself, causing them to find Him within. This is the beginning of the inward, or deeper life.

As soon as this change takes place, He then teaches, if He can make them to get it, either by teachers or by their light, how to "practice the presence of God" – that is, to keep the mind *stayed* on Jesus – each wandering thought, act, work, or feeling being recalled (i.e., called back) by the will of the vessel in the love of God.

However, this takes care. Often the mind lingers over a subject not of God. Turn the mind back to God. Words come not appointed by Him. Check such words at once, as soon as remembered. Look within and tell Jesus He rules, you will act, think, and speak as He would and He will look after you to help you to be like that.

Also, you need to watch and pray to be in God, wait in God, etc. To so live for a time makes the inward change to abide in anyone who will go down to thus live; but if you keep to this lowliness, rest, and faith to be all the time in God so, then the voluntary act of dwelling in God, seeing God, thinking of God, and keeping in God is done altogether by the Holy Ghost, which is the true inwardness called for in every Christian.

Martha Wing Robinson

V. THE PURPOSE

What is the purpose of cultivating the "inner life message"? Always remember, it's the inward for the outward. In other words, we cultivate the beauty of this reflective, contemplative prayer life to give us riches to export to others through rightfully motivated deeds of kindness and demonstrations of God's power.

Yes, it's the inward for the outward! Let us search out the treasures of *Christ in us the hope of glory* and then release displays of His brilliant presence wherever we go. So I invite you to go on a journey with me on a road less traveled. Let's seek out together the treasures of the Inward Journey as the beginning steps into consecrated, contemplative prayer.

Reflection Questions
Lesson One: The Inward for the Outward

Answers to these questions can be found in the back of the study guide.

Fill in the Blank

1. Isaiah 30:15 – *In _____ and _____ shall be your strength.*

2. What three things were placed inside the Ark of the Covenant?
   1. _____ 2. _____ 3. _____

3. John 14:20 – *And in that day you shall know that I am in the _____, and you are in _____ and I _____ you.*

Multiple Choice – Choose the best answer from the list below:

A.	Jesus	C.	Temple
B.	House	D.	Presence

4. I Corinthians 3:16 – *Do you not know that you are a _____ of God and that the Spirit of God dwells in you?*

5. Practicing His _____ is constantly staying our eyes upon Jesus.

True or False

6. The inward journey is an invitation to enter into the depths of Jesus Christ. _____

7. Doorways like Forgiveness, Cleansing, Grace, and Mercy are all vital to achieving union with God. _____

8. Cultivating an inward life is the very expression of who we are in Christ. _____

Scripture Memorization

9. Write out and memorize I Corinthians 6:16-19 on the next page.

10. What was the primary point you learned from this lesson?

Lesson Two:
What True Communion Requires – Part One

I.   THE CONTEMPLATIVE LESSONS

True intimacy with God cannot be fully realized without **quietness** of body, soul, and spirit. An atmosphere of stillness is absolutely essential for the believer in Jesus to enter into the experience of His deep, communing love.

In order for us to hear His still, small voice within us, we must become quiet. Psalm 46:10 tells us, *"Be still and know that I am God".* Other translations of that verse are: *cease striving, let go, relax, and know that I am God.* This "knowing" goes far beyond informational knowledge. Rather, it is His Spirit in union with ours. His breath in us. His heart in our heart. This "knowing" is inseparable with the spirit of revelation that causes us to "know" and thus experience our true union with Christ.

Often we miss the imperative of quieting ourselves as we approach God. Our lives are in such a rush. We just run up to God, blurt out our prayers, and rush away again. I am convinced we will never fully enter His presence in such a way.

Mark Virkler in his book, *Communion with God,* states - "Stillness is not a goal in itself. I want to become still in my mind and body so my heart can know and sense God moving within. His promptings are gentle, and until my own inner and outer ragings are quieted, I will not sense His inner moving." [2]

The psalmist David summed it up when he wrote, *Rest in the Lord; wait patiently for Him to act...don't fret or worry...all who humble themselves before the Lord shall be given many blessings, and shall have wonderful peace.* (Psa. 37:7, 8, 11 TLB)

Quietness is not a new discovery or a recent innovation. It isn't even a new slant on an old discovery! It is a time-honored and proven method of fellowshipping with God that is almost totally ignored by modern-day Christians.

This type of contemplative waiting is, of course, just one of the expressions of prayer. It is not a quick fix to all our problems. It is, however, one neglected weapon in God's arsenal that will help us find His path through life's perplexing maze.

II. LESSONS ON QUIETING OUR SOUL [3]

A. From the Writings of Madame Jeanne Guyon (1648-1717)

Much of her life was spent in confinement and prison in France, due to her religious beliefs. Her devotional writings compel the reader to move into a living experience of Jesus Christ. *Experiencing the Depths of Jesus Christ* greatly influenced Watchman Nee, John Wesley, Hudson Taylor, and is still one of the widely read classics of our day.

1. **Beholding the Lord**
   In "beholding the Lord", you come to the Lord in a totally different way. Perhaps at this point I need to share with you the greatest difficulty you will have in waiting upon the Lord. It has to do with your mind. The mind has a very strong tendency to stray away from the Lord. Therefore, as you come before the Lord to sit in His presence...beholding Him, make use of the scripture to quiet your mind. The way to do this is really quite simple. First, read a passage of scripture. Once you sense the Lord's presence, the content of what you have read is no longer important. The scripture has served its purpose: it has quieted your mind and brought you to Him.

2. **Distractions**
   What about distractions? Let's say that your mind begins to wander. Once you have been deeply touched by the Lord's Spirit and are distracted, be diligent to bring your wandering mind back to the Lord. This is the easiest way in the world to overcome external distractions.

   When your mind has wandered, don't try to deal with it by changing what you are thinking. You see, if you pay attention to what you are thinking, you will only irritate your mind and stir it up more! Instead, withdraw from your mind! Keep turning within to the Lord's presence. By doing this, you will win the war with your wandering mind and yet never directly engage in the battle!

3. **Disciplining the Mind**
   As you begin this venture you will, of course, discover that it is difficult to bring your mind under control. Why is this? Because through many years of habit, your mind has acquired the ability to wander all over the world, just as it pleases, so what I speak of here is something that is to serve as a discipline to your mind.

   Be assured that as your soul becomes more accustomed to withdrawing to inward things, this process will become easier.

There are two reasons that you will find it easier each time to bring your mind under subjection to the Lord: first of all, the mind – after much practice – will form a new habit of turning deep within; secondly, you have a gracious Lord!

B. From the Writings of Henry Nouwen (1932 - 1996) [4]

Born in Holland, he came to the U. S. in 1964. He was a Catholic priest and psychologist who has taught at numerous universities and authored such titles as *The Wounded Healer* and *The Road to Daybreak*. The following selection from *Making All Things New* invites us to intimate spiritual life.

1. Inner Chaos

To bring some solitude into our lives is one of the most necessary but also most difficult disciplines. Even though we may have a deep desire for real solitude, we also experience a certain apprehension as we approach that solitary place and time. As soon as we are alone, without people to talk with, a book to read, TV to watch, or phone calls to make, an inner chaos opens up in us.

This chaos can be so disturbing and so confusing that we can hardly wait to get busy again! Entering a private room and shutting the door, therefore, doesn't mean that we immediately shut out all of our inner doubts, anxieties, fears, bad memories, unresolved conflicts, angry feelings and impulsive desires. On the contrary, when we have removed our outer distractions, we often find that our outer distractions manifest themselves to us in full force!

We often use these outer distractions to shield ourselves from interior noises. It is thus not surprising that we have a difficult time being alone. The confrontation with our inner conflicts can be too painful for us to endure. This makes the discipline of solitude all the more important! Solitude is not a spontaneous response to an occupied and preoccupied life. There are too many reasons not to be alone. Therefore, we must begin by carefully planning some solitude.

2. Bombarded by Thousands of Thoughts

Once we have committed ourselves to spending time in solitude, we develop an attentiveness to God's voice in us. In the beginning, during the first days, weeks, or even months, we may have the feeling that we are simply wasting our time. Time in "quietness" may at first seem a little more than a time in which we are bombarded by thousands of thoughts and feelings that emerge from hidden areas of our minds.

One of the early Christian writers describes the first stages of solitary prayer as the experience of a man who, after many years of living with open doors, suddenly decides to shut them. The visitors who used to come and enter start pounding on his doors, wondering why they are not allowed to enter. Only when they realize that they are not welcome do they gradually stop coming.

This is the experience of anyone who decides to enter into solitude after a life without much spiritual discipline. At first, the many distractions keep presenting themselves. Later, as they receive less and less attention, they slowly withdraw.

3. **The Way to Hope**
    The discipline of solitude allows us to come in touch with this hopeful presence of God in our lives and allows us to also taste, even now, the beginnings of joy and peace which belong to the new heaven and the new earth.

    This discipline, as I have described it here, is one of the most powerful disciplines in developing a prayer life. It is a simple, though not easy, way to free us from the slavery of our occupations and preoccupations and to begin to hear that voice that makes all things new.

C. **From the Writings of Jean Nicholas Grou (1730–1803)** [5]

He lived in Holland and France and was a Jesuit priest who entered into a deeper life with God on a retreat in 1767, where he learned to live his life in the spirit of prayer and complete abandonment to God's will. The following passage comes from his famous book, *How to Pray.*

1. **The Voice of the Heart**
    You ask me what this voice of the heart is. It is love which is the voice of the heart. Love God and you will always be speaking to Him. The seed of love is growth in prayer. If you do not understand that, you have never yet either loved or prayed. Ask God to open your heart and kindle in it a spark of His love and then you will begin to understand what praying means.

    If it is the heart that prays, it is evident that sometimes, and even continuously, it can pray by itself without any help from words, spoken or conceived. Here is something which few people understand and which some even entirely deny. They insist that there must be definite and formal acts. They are mistaken, and God has not yet taught them how the heart prays. It is true that the thoughts are formed in the mind before they are clothed in words. The proof of this is that we often search for the right word and reject one after another until we find the right one which expresses our thoughts accurately.

We need words to make ourselves intelligible to other people but not to the Spirit. It is the same with the feelings of the heart. The heart conceives feelings and adopts them without any need of resorting to words, unless it wishes to communicate them to others or to make them clear to itself. For God reads the secrets of the heart. God reads its most intimate feelings, even those that we are not aware of. It is not necessary to make use of formal acts to make ourselves heard by God. If we do make use of them in prayer, it is not so much for God's sake as our own, in that they keep our attention fixed in His presence.

2. **The Prayer of Silence**
Imagine a soul so closely united to God that it has no need of outward acts to remain attentive to the inward prayer. In these moments of silence and peace, when it pays no heed to what is happening within itself, it prays and prays excellently with a simple and direct prayer that God will understand perfectly by the action of grace. The heart will be full as aspirations towards God without any clear expression. Though they may elude our own consciousness, they will not escape the consciousness of God.

This prayer, so empty of all images and perceptions...apparently so passive and yet so active, is - as far as the limitations of this life allow - pure adoration in spirit and in truth. It is adoration fully worthy of God in which the soul is united to Him as its ground, the created intelligence to the uncreated, without anything but a very simple attention of the mind and as equally simple application of the will. This is what is called the prayer of silence, or quiet, or of bare faith.

D.   From the Writings of Andrew Murray [6]

He was a gifted nineteenth century Dutch Reformed pastor who was born in South Africa in 1828. After receiving his education in Scotland and Holland, he returned to South Africa where he spent many years pastoring, teaching, and writing. He was a staunch advocate for biblical Christianity. He is best known for his book, *With Christ in the School of Prayer*. The following are excerpts from his classic, *Waiting on God*.

1.   **Quietness and Faith**
Take heed and be quiet; fear not, neither be faint-hearted. In quietness and confidence shall be your strength. Such words reveal to us the close connection between quietness and faith. They show us what a deep need there is of quietness, as an element of true waiting upon God. If we are to have our whole heart turned toward God, we must have it turned away from man, from all that occupies and interests, whether joy or sorrow. The message is one of deep meaning – *take heed and be quiet.*

2.   **An Unspeakable Blessedness**
As long as the waiting on God is chiefly regarded as an end towards more effectual prayer, and the obtaining of our petitions, this spirit of perfect quietness will not be obtained. But when it is seen that waiting on God is, in itself, an unspeakable blessedness – one of the highest forms of fellowship with the Holy One – the adoration of Him in His glory will of necessity humble the soul into holy stillness, making way for God to speak and reveal Himself. Then it comes to the fulfillment of the precious promise that all of self and self-effort will be humbled. "The haughtiness of man shall be brought down and the Lord alone shall be exalted in that day."

3.   **It Will Come**
Though at first it may appear difficult to know how thus quietly to wait, with the activities of the mind and heart for a time subdued, every effort after it will be rewarded. We will discover that it grows upon us and the little season of silent worship will bring a peace and a rest that give a blessing not only in prayer, but all day!

4.   **It is Good!**

It is good that a man should...quietly wait for the salvation of the Lord. Yes, it is good! It will not be done with our willing and running, with all our thinking and praying. It is the confession of our desire to sink into our nothingness and to let Him work and reveal Himself. Do let us wait quietly. In daily life, let there be in the soul that is waiting for the great God to do His wondrous work a quiet reverence and an abiding watching against too deep of an engrossment with the world. Then the whole character will come to bear the beautiful stamp: quietly waiting for the salvation of God!

Reflection Questions
Lesson Two: What True Communion Requires – Part One

Answers to these questions can be found in the back of the study guide.

Fill in the Blank

1. Being "still" can mean _____ _____ _____

2. This "knowing" of God is His Spirit in _____ with ours.

3. List distractions that you need to shut out in order to quiet your soul before God. _____
   _____

Multiple Choice – Choose the best answer from the list below:

A.	Secrets	C.	Weapon
B.	Life	D.	Banner

4. Contemplative prayer is a _____ in God's arsenal that helps us through life's perplexing maze.

5. God reads the _____ of the heart, and know the most intimate feelings, even those we are not aware of.

True or False

6. It is good that a man should quietly wait for the salvation of the Lord. _____

7. Waiting on God is chiefly regarded as end toward more effectual prayer and obtaining your petitions. _____

8. One needs outward acts to remain attentive to God. _____

Scripture Memorization

9. Write out and memorize Psalm 37:7-11.

10. What was the primary point you learned from this lesson?

Lesson Three:
What True Communion Requires – Part Two

I. THE COMBATIVE LESSONS ON QUIETING OUR SOUL

A. From the Writings of Mark Virkler [7]

He is a pastor-teacher based in Buffalo, New York. Mark has written 30 study manuals in the areas of Bible survey and spiritual communion and growth. The following thoughts are contained in his powerful book, *Communion with God.*

1. **Principles of Communion**

   If we are going to commune with God, first we must become still. Habakkuk went to his guard post to pray (Hab. 2:1). In the early morning when it was still dark, Jesus departed to a lonely place to pray (Mk. 1:35). And after a day's ministry, Jesus went to a mountain to pray.

   In order for our inner man to commune with God, we must first remove external distractions. We must find a place where we can be alone and undisturbed so that we can center down into our hearts without being distracted by our external circumstances.

   Second, we must learn to quiet our inner being, all the voices and thoughts within us that are calling for our attention. Until they are quieted, we most likely will not hear His voice.

   Becoming still cannot be hurried or forced. Rather, it must be allowed to happen. At a point in your stillness, God takes over and you sense His active flow within you. His spontaneous images begin to flow with a life of their own. His voice speaks, giving you wisdom and strength. You find that you are *in the Spirit* (Rev. 1:10).

2. **Quieting Our Own Inner Being**

   a) Write down thoughts of things to do later
   b) Release present tensions and anxieties to the Lord
   c) Focus on Jesus
   d) In becoming still, I am not trying to do anything. I simply want to be in touch with the Divine Lover. I am centered on this moment of time and experiencing Him in it.
   e) Removing inner noise (voices, thoughts, pressures).

3. **Problems and Solutions**

Problem	Solution
Thoughts of things to do	Write them down so you won't forget
Thoughts of sin-consciousness	Confess your sin and clothe yourself with the robe of righteousness
Mind flitting about	Speak to your mind - say "no!" Focus on a vision of Jesus with you.
Difficulty getting in touch	Begin singing in tongues and listen with your heart to spontaneous song bubbling up from your heart
Need more time!	Realize that times when you are doing automatic activities (driving, bathing, exercising, washing dishes, etc.) are ideal times to hear from God.

B. **The Battlefield of the Mind**

1. **Taking an Aggressive Posture**
    II Cor. 10:2-5 – *For the weapons of our warfare are not of the flesh, but divinely powerful for the destruction of fortresses. We are destroying speculations and every lofty thing raised up against the knowledge of God, and we are taking every thought captive to the obedience of Christ.*

    As I read this set of scriptures, I envision this "battlefield of the mind" in a specific way. I see these strongholds or fortresses (vs. 4) as being the ancient wall around our mind. These strongholds are our overall mental attitude. Next, I envision the arguments or speculations (vs. 5) as being the guards on the wall of human reasoning. The high or lofty things (vs. 5) are the high towers on the wall called pride. Lastly, the thoughts (vs. 5) are the individuals of military might, poised for battle with devices of the power of suggestion.

2. **Taking the Initiative**
    Our weapons are not carnal but they are mighty in God for the pulling down of strongholds, casting down of arguments and every high thing that exalts itself against the knowledge of Christ. Through the "Battering Ram" of the name of Jesus, the blood (Rev. 12:11), and God's written and spoken word (Mt. 4:3-10), we can bring every thought into obedience to Christ Jesus.

3. **Practical Steps**

Before we can think on *whatsoever things are true, noble, just, pure, lovely, of a good report, full of virtue and praise* (Phil. 4:7,8), we must first cleanse our minds. This does not happen overnight. But for the Christian, it is a part of their destiny.

Some steps to having the mind of Christ might include:

a) Confession –I John 1:7-9
b) Forgiving – Prov. 14:10
c) Forgetting – Phil. 3:13
d) Removing – Heb. 12:1; II Cor. 6:17
e) Combating and withstanding – II Cor. 10:2-6
f) Building up – I Pet. 1:13; Jas. 1:21; Isa. 28:11; Jude 20
g) Putting on – I Thes. 5:8; Prov. 16:3; Eph. 4:17-24

II.   CONCLUDING THOUGHTS

A.   From the Writings of Dallas Willard [8]

He is a professor and past director of the School of Philosophy at the University of Southern California. Dallas is the author of the penetrating book, *The Spirit of the Disciplines*, of which the following is taken.

A discipline for the spiritual life is, when the dust of history is blown away, nothing but an activity undertaken to bring us into more effective cooperation with Christ and His kingdom. As with all disciplines, we should approach the practice of silence in a prayerful, experimental attitude, confident that we shall be led into its right use for us. It is a powerful and essential discipline.

Only silence will allow us life-transforming concentration upon God. It allow us to hear the gentle God, whose only Son *shall not strive, nor cry; neither shall any man hear His voice above the street noise* (Mt. 12:19). It is this God who tells us that *in quietness and trust is your strength* (Isa. 30:15).

B.   From the Writings of Mary Ruth Swope [9]

Mary Swope, author of *Are You Sick and Tired of Feeling Sick and Tired*, turns her attention to helping people understand how to hear and discern God's voice. The following phrases are from her book, *Listening Prayer*.

1. **Beginning**

    At the beginning of each period of listening prayer, submit yourself to God and invite the Holy Spirit to be in control. Learn to "put you mind on the shelf." If your thoughts begin to seep through, you will block the Holy Spirit's willingness to speak through your mind.

2. **The Attacks**

    In addition, Satan will try to distract you. Cast out any interfering thoughts from the enemy. The clamoring images and mindset of the world will drown out the quiet inner promptings of the Holy Spirit.

3. **Rest in Him!**

    Sit back and enjoy God's presence. Meditate on His power, His wisdom, His goodness, His meekness, and His generosity. Let His peace flow through you and feel the serenity of mind and heart that illuminates and invigorates. His Spirit gives strength to any task that needs to be accomplished.

    Relax and release all tension. Anxiety and strain will evoke only silence from God. Learn to let go and let God speak to you. Only those who retreat to the quietness of heart, mind, and spirit can hear God's voice and receive direct inspiration.

C. From the Words of Jesus in Matthew 6:5-6

*And when you pray, you must not be like the hypocrites; for they love to stand and pray in the synagogues and at the street corners, that they may be seen by men. Truly, I say to you, they have their reward. But when you pray, **go into your room and shut the door** and pray to your Father who is in secret, and your Father who sees in secret will reward you.*

D. From the Psalmist in Psalm 62:5

My soul, wait in silence for God only. For my hope is from Him.

<u>A simple prayer</u>: Father, lead me into these forgotten ways. Silence the inner raging of voices contending for my attention. Quiet my soul that I might know you and your precious Son Jesus. Holy Spirit, take your liberty to write these laws in my heart. Lord, I want to know you. Teach me for your kingdom's sake. Amen!

Reflection Questions
Lesson Three: What True Communion Requires – Part Two

Answers to these questions can be found in the back of the study guide.

Fill in the Blank

1. Habakkuk 2:1 – *I will stand on my _____ _____ and station myself on the rampart and I will _____ _____ to see what He will speak to me and how I may reply when I am reproved.*

2. Mark 1:35 – *And in the early morning...He arose and went out and departed to a _____ _____, and was _____ there.*

3. Some steps to having the mind of Christ are 1. _____ 2. _____ 3. _____ 4. _____

Multiple Choice – Choose the best answer from the list below:

A.	Devises	C.	Weapons
B.	Room	D.	House

4. Matthew 6:6 – *But you, when you pray, go into your _____, and when you have shut the door, pray to thy Father...*

5. Our _____ are not carnal, but mighty in God.

True or False

6. Silence causes distractions from hearing the voice of God. _____

7. The strongholds of warfare are in the mind. _____

8. "Thoughts to do" pose problems that can be solved by writing them down. _____

Scripture Memorization

9. Write out and memorize I Corinthians 10:4-5.

10. What was the primary point you learned from this lesson?

Lesson Four:
Listening, Waiting and Watching in Prayer

I. LAYING THE FOUNDATION

A. Primary Verse and Emphasis

1. Proverbs 8:32-36
   Now therefore, O sons, listen to me, for blessed are they who keep my ways. Heed instruction and be wise. And do not neglect it. Blessed is the man who listens to me, watching daily at my gates, waiting at my doorposts. For he who finds me finds life, and obtains favor from the Lord. But he who sins against me injures himself; all those who hate me love death.

2. Three key words are in the passive, continuous tense.
   a) listen
   b) watching
   c) waiting

3. The promise is verse 35
   a) when you find Me you find life!
   b) you will obtain favor from the Lord.
   But how do you find Him?

B. From the Life of Joshua

1. Exodus 17:8-13
   Aaron and Hur held up the hands of Moses and as they did, Joshua would win the battle in the field. (This shows the life of the warrior is tied to the power of intercession and praise, i.e. uplifted hands and arms.)

2. Exodus 33:7-11
   While all the other people would return to their own tents and carry out their own "business as usual" young Joshua would wait at the entrance of the tent of meeting. He would be the first to see the reflection of God's glory and Moses' face. This positioning of ourselves at the feet of Jesus; this listening, waiting, and watching will do this for us as well. We will see the face of Jesus and the radiance of God's light shall shine upon us.

C. From the Life of David

1. Psalms 84:1-12, especially 84:10
   For a day in Thy courts is better than a thousand outside. I would rather stand at the threshold of the house of my God, than dwell in the tents of wickedness. (I would rather be a doorkeeper.)
2. David knew the art of waiting at the threshold of the door of the house of God. This is the art of listening, waiting and watching.

II. LISTENING

A. Primary Verse

1. Isaiah 50:4,5
   The Lord God has given me the tongue of disciples, that I may know how to sustain the weary one with a word. He awakens me morning by morning. He awakens my ear to listen as a disciple. The Lord God has opened my ear; and I was not disobedient, nor did I turn back.
2. Pray these verses over your own life. Ask that you be given a listening ear.
3. We do not each "hear" in the same manner. (See other Lessons on the Multi-Faceted Voice of God in the study guide, *Receiving and Discerning Revelation* and the lesson "Practical Suggestions to Hearing His Voice", in the study guide, *Prophetic Foundations.*

B. Mark 9:1-8 – The Transfiguration

1. Mark 9:7, 8
   Then, a cloud formed overshadowing them and a voice came out of the cloud, "This is My beloved Son, listen to Him!" And all at once they looked around and saw no one with them any more, except Jesus only.
2. These scriptures depict the jealousy of the Father for His Son. It demonstrates His great longing to speak to us.
3. They saw no one any more, except Jesus. In order to hear God, we must learn to deal with distraction. The key is to be so focused on Him that everything else fades in the background.
4. They could have gotten caught up in lengthy discussions of the past or present moves of God (Moses - the Law; and Elijah - the prophets). But the Father directed their eyes to see Jesus only.
5. We need a revelation of His loveliness. This is a higher path than just resisting evil. When will see and know His love, then we will stop and listen.

C. **Luke 19:45-48 – Listening in the Temple**

1.   Verse 48
And they could not find anything that they might do, for all the people were hanging upon His words.

2.   May a corporate people in our day emerge who will press in daily and listen to His every word. A promise of protection awaits such a people.

D. **Obstacles to Hearing God's Voice**
There are at least seven reasons why Christians today do not hear from God on a regular (even daily) basis. They are:

1.   Lack of faith to believe that hearing from God is for today.
2.   Lack of a commitment to Jesus Christ as Lord of their life.
3.   The presence of unconfessed sin and a "double-standard" lifestyle.
4.   Ignorance of the scriptural evidence of the believer's privilege to hear from God personally.
5.   Lack of teaching on how to pursue such a listening prayer experience.
6.   Fear of being called a "religious fanatic" or "mentally ill."
7.   Fear of being open to the "wrong spirits" or being led astray by the enemy.

E. **Assurance that God is Speaking**
If you can respond to the following statements affirmatively, then rest assured that God is speaking to you:

1.   What I heard helps me to respect (fear) the Lord and to depart from evil (Job 28:28).
2.   The message increases my faith in or my knowledge and understanding of scripture (Prov. 4:7).
3.   The actions that will result from following this will be full of spiritual fruits: purity, peace, gentleness, mercy, courtesy, good deeds, sincerity, and without hypocrisy (Jas 3:17).
4.   What I heard strengthens me "with all might" so that I can keep going no matter what happens (Col. 1:1).
5.   It causes me to experience joyfulness and thanksgiving to the Father (Col. 1:12).

III.   WAITING

A.   Primary Verses

1.   Isaiah 30:18-21
Therefore the Lord longs to be gracious to you, and therefore He waits on high to have compassion on you. For the Lord is a God of justice: How blessed are all those who long for Him. O people in Zion, inhabitants in Jerusalem, you will weep no longer. He will surely be gracious to you at the sound of your cry; when He hears it, He will answer you. Although the Lord has given you bread of privation and water of oppression, He, your Teacher will no longer hide Himself, but your eyes will behold your Teacher, and your ears will hear a word behind you, "This is the way, walk in it," whenever you turn to the right or to the left.

2.   He waits for us. He longs for us. He has compassion towards us. He comes running when He hears our voice!

B.   Other Scriptures from Isaiah

1.   Isaiah 64:1-4
Neither has the eye seen a God besides Thee, Who acts in behalf of the one who waits for Him.

2.   Isaiah 40:31
Those who wait for the Lord will gain new strength; they will mount up with wings as eagles, they will run and not get tired. They will walk and not become weary.

3.   Initiative is the issue. In the book of Acts it is not God following man, but man waiting on God and then men trying to keep up with what God is doing.

C.   From the Writings of Andrew Murray – Waiting on God [10]

And therefore will the Lord wait, that He may be gracious unto you, and therefore will He be exalted, that He may have mercy upon you: for the Lord is a God of judgment: blessed are all they that wait for Him - Isaiah 30:8

We must not only think of our waiting upon God, but also of what is more wonderful still, of God's waiting upon us. The vision of Him waiting on us will give new impulse and inspiration to our waiting upon Him. It will give us an unspeakable confidence that our waiting cannot be in vain. If He waits for us, then we may be sure that we are more than welcome – that He rejoices to find those He has been seeking for. Let us seek even now, at this moment, in the spirit of lowly waiting on God, to find out something of what it means.

Therefore will the Lord wait, that He may be gracious unto you. We will accept and echo back the message: *Blessed are all they that wait for Him.*

Look up and see the great God upon His throne. He is love - and unceasing and inexpressible desire to communicate His own goodness and blessedness to all His creatures. He longs and delights to bless. He has inconceivably glorious purposes concerning every one of His children, by the power of His Holy Spirit, to reveal in them His love and power. He waits with all the longings of a father's heart. He waits that He may be gracious unto you. And, each time you come to wait upon Him, or seek to maintain in daily life the holy habit of waiting, you may look up and see Him ready to meet you. He will be waiting so that He may be gracious unto you. Yes, connect every exercise, every breath of the life of waiting, with faith's vision of your God waiting for you.

And if you ask: How is it, if He waits to be gracious, that even after I come and wait upon Him, He does not give the help I seek, but waits on longer and longer? There is a double answer. The one is this. God is a wise husbandman, *who waiteth for the precious fruit of the earth, and hath long patience for it.* He cannot gather the fruit until it is ripe. He knows when we are spiritually ready to receive the blessing to our profit and His glory.

Waiting in the sunshine of His love is what will ripen the soul for His blessing. Waiting under the cloud of trail that breaks in showers of blessing is as needful. Be assured that if God waits longer than you could wish, it is only to make the blessing doubly precious. God waited four thousand years until the fullness of time, before He sent His Son. Our times are in His hands. He will avenge His elect speedily. He will make haste for our help, and not delay one hour too long.

The other answer points to what has been said before. The giver is more than the gift; God is more than the blessing. And, our being kept waiting on Him is the only way for our learning to find our life and joy in Himself. Oh, if God's children only knew what a glorious God they have, and what a privilege it is to be linked in fellowship with Him, then they would rejoice in Him! Even when He keeps them waiting, they will learn to understand better than ever. *Therefore will the Lord wait, that He may be gracious unto you.* His waiting will be the highest proof of His graciousness.

Blessed are all they that wait for Him. A queen has her ladies-in-waiting. The position is one of subordination and service, and yet it is considered one of the highest dignity and privilege, because a wise and gracious sovereign makes them companions and friends. What a dignity and blessedness to be attendants-in-waiting on the everlasting God, ever on the watch for every indication of His will or favor, ever conscious of His nearness, His goodness, and His grace! *The Lord is good to them that wait for Him. Blessed are all they that wait for Him.* Yet, it is blessed when a waiting soul and a waiting God meet each other. God cannot do His work without His and our waiting His time. Let waiting be our work, as it is His. And, if His waiting is nothing but goodness and graciousness, let ours be nothing but a rejoicing in that goodness, and a confident expectancy of that grace. And, let every thought of waiting become to us the simple expression of unmingled and unutterable blessedness, because it brings us to a God who waits that He may make Himself known to us perfectly as the gracious One. My soul, wait thou only upon God!

IV.   WATCHING

A.   Primary Verse

1.   Habakkuk 2:1-3
     I will stand on my guard post and station myself on the rampart; and I will keep watch to see what He will speak to me and how I may reply when I am reproved. Then the Lord answered me and said, 'Record the vision and inscribe it on tablets, that the one who reads it may run. For the vision is yet for the appointed time; it hastens toward the goal, and it will not fail. Though it tarries, wait for it; for it will certainly come, it will not delay.'
2.   The proper inner attitude is the key that unlocks our ability to hear and see in the Spirit.
3.   "Watching" is both a gift and an art that is learned. This is a combination then, of gifting and character development.

B.   Isaiah 62:6,7

1.   Habakkuk 2:1
     I will stand on my guard post and station myself on the rampart; and I will keep watch to see what He will speak to me.

2. There are two primary tasks of these guard-watchmen
   a) They are to guard, resist, and warn. These watchmen are to alert the people and to keep the enemy out.
   b) These watchers are to receive and permit the "ambassadors" to come in.

C. Matthew 26:38

1. Jesus said, *"Could you not tarry (watch) with me for an hour?"*
2. It does not just say, "Pray!" Instead, it says to "watch." This is a very important posture to learn in our praying!

D. Ezekiel 33:6

1. But if the watchman sees the sword coming and does not blow the trumpet, and the people are not warned, and a sword comes and takes a person from them, he is taken away in his iniquity; but his blood I will require from the watchman's hand.
2. One of the greatest prophetic words given to me was a picture sent to me from Paul Cain and Reed Graftke of a man who had fallen asleep on his watch on the wall. Hordes of enemies were approaching to take the "city" as the watcher was asleep. This scripture from Ezekiel 33:6 is written out on the picture and is a constant reminder to me to be alert on my watch for and with Him.

V. LET US BE ALERT!

Let us learn the lessons of the ongoing activity of listening, waiting and watching. As we commit ourselves to these skills we will *truly find Him and obtain favor from the Lord.* Let us be alert and learn the arts of communion with our Master.

Reflection Questions
Lesson Four: Listening, Waiting and Watching in Prayer

Answers to these questions can be found in the back of the study guide.

Fill in the Blank

1. Proverbs 8:34 – *Blessed is the man who* _____ *to me.* _____ *daily at my gates.* _____ *at the doorposts. For he who finds me finds life.*

2. Joshua would wait at the entrance to the _____ of _____.

3. List four of the seven obstacles to hearing God's voice on a regular basis.

   1. _____   2. _____
   3. _____   4. _____

Multiple Choice – Choose the best answer from the list below:

A.	Waits	C.	Watchman
B.	Elders	D.	Longs

4. _____ are to alert the people, so the enemy is kept out.

5. Isaiah 64:4 – *Neither has the eye seen a God besides thee, who acts on behalf of the one who* _____ *for Him.*

True or False

6. In the book of Acts, it is God following man, not man waiting on God. _____

7. If the watchman sees the sword coming and does not blow the trumpet, any bloodshed will be required of him. _____

8. The Lord is good to those who wait on Him. _____

Scripture Memorization

9. Write out and memorize Isaiah 40: 29-31

10. What was the primary point you learned from this lesson?

Section Two:

Contemplative Prayer

Lesson Five:
Contemplative Prayer – What It Is Not

I.   INTRODUCTION

A.   An Invitation Was Granted

1.   **A Dream** – "I will reveal the hidden streams of the prophetic to you." This was spoken to me in a dream from the Lord in 1991. This was an invitation from the Holy Spirit into fresh understandings of "old" revelatory ways.
2.   **A Word** – "I will teach you to release the highest weapon of spiritual warfare - the brilliance of My Great Presence." This word came in October, 1994 while resting in the Lord.

B.   My Personal Journey
As I began to walk in these overlooked pathways in my Christian experience I found:

1.   It was a road less traveled.
2.   Reading the Desert Fathers and writings of others were valuable guideposts for my journey.
3.   Encouragement came from others as I talked with experienced, older saints.
4.   I found it to be a road on which I was already somewhat familiar.

II.   A BRIEF GLANCE AT CONTEMPLATIVE PRAYER

A.   Key Scriptures

1.   II Cor. 3:18 – *But we all, with unveiled face beholding as in a mirror the glory of the Lord, are being transformed into the same image from glory to glory, just as from the Lord, the Spirit.*
2.   Psalm 46:10 – *Cease striving and know that I am God; I will be exalted among the nations, I will be exalted in the earth.*
3.   Heb. 12:2 – *Fixing our eyes on Jesus, the author and perfecter of faith, who for the joy set before Him, endured the cross, despising the shame, and has sat down at the right hand of the throne of God.*

B. What Is Prayer?

There are many types of prayer or focuses of prayer. This is not intercession but may lead to it.

Prayer is not doing something, but being with Someone. It is communion with God himself. We are to continue in prayer until we become one with Him. As we continue in "being with Him", we come into a greater "oneness" with Him and eventually an expression of Jesus emanates forth.

C. A Synopsis

We do not intrinsically become Jesus, but when we have set our gaze upon Him (Heb. 12:2) with loving affection for so long, we become a reflection of His glory (II Cor. 3:18), taking on His character (Gal. 5:22,23) and His power (I Cor. 12:7-11). A union has taken place in our spirits (I Cor. 6:17), and we have become joined to Him and Him to us. Gal. 2:20 - *It is no longer I who live, but Christ who lives in me.*

III. CONTEMPLATIVE PRAYER IS NOT

A. It Is Not:

1. A technique.
2. A relaxation therapy exercise.
3. A form of self-hypnosis or mesmerism.
4. A para-psychological phenomenon.
5. A "New Age" approach to improve ourselves.
6. An attempt to make the mind blank or make us "empty-headed."
7. A "new thing" or a remake of Eastern meditation.

B. Difference between Contemplative Prayer and Eastern Meditation [11]
Adapted from a teaching by Dr. Steve Meeks – Calvary Community Church, Houston Texas:

1. Eastern methods are primarily concerned with "awareness." Contemplative prayer is concerned with divine love between God and a person.
2. Eastern traditions put the greater emphasis on what self can do. Christian tradition recognizes that our unique individuality was created by God and for God as a vehicle for His expression in the world.
3. Eastern methods seek to get in touch with man's spiritual nature by concentrating on a mantra or some other method of forced concentration. Contemplative prayer presupposes a

personal relationship. Contemplative prayer encompasses a voluntary desire to get in touch with our spiritual nature.

4. Eastern methods focus on what a person can do through focused concentration. Contemplative prayer focuses on surrendering to what only God can do.

5. Contemplative prayer is not a relaxation exercise such breathing techniques or yoga. It is a faith relationship where we open ourselves to our living, personal, loving Father God.

C. Distinctions between Christian Contemplative Prayer and New Age Thought [12]

1. An Overview

The "New Age Movement" appears to be a loosely knit group of individuals and organizations who believe that we have entered a "New Age" called the "age of Aquarius." This age has allegedly replaced the Age of Pisces, which some say represents the Christian era (Pisces - fish - the early Christian symbol.) The Age of Aquarius (water bearer) is characterized by humanism, brother-hood and supposed love. It is to be a so-called "golden age."

We recognize that New Agers are part of the great counterfeit that may use words, phrases, and techniques that have been borrowed from Christianity and then tainted. Yet we will not give over either these words or these experiences to be the sole possession of the satanic counterfeit, as they are God's.

For example, New Agers have borrowed the rainbow, which, of course, was part of God's covenant with Noah. They have also stolen the term "centering" which is a word and an experience that has for decades been used by the Christian group, the Quakers.

We have a standard, the Word of God, and our acceptance of a truth is not based on whether or not a counterfeit group has distorted it. We look to see if it is taught in scripture; and surely such things as the concept of centering and quieting our souls before the Lord is clearly taught and demonstrated by King David in Psalms 62:1, 5 where it states, *My soul waits in silence for God only.*

Therefore, we will expect the New Age to blur the line between truth and error through their eclectic nature. But we shall concern ourselves with encountering fully and completely the God of the authoritative Judeo-Christian scriptures.

The New Age has arisen to take the territory abandoned by mainstream Christianity. Because Christianity has neglected the initiative and relational and has majored on the propositional and the analytical, a void has been left in the hearts of those who were seeking spiritual encounters. This is certainly no time to draw back from supernatural living and retreat.

Since the dawn of history, whenever people do not preach, proclaim, and model the genuine article, men and women will wander into whatever appears to offer fulfillment of their spiritual quest. We need to cast aside our hesitation and proceed strongly forward with the Word and the Holy Spirit as our unfailing guide!

The New Age is but Satan's reaction to the mighty outpouring of the Holy Spirit that we are seeing in this century. I do not see it as something to fear or from which to flee. Since when does light fear darkness? No, I must stand against it in the power of the Holy Spirit and re-claim the land of meditation, contemplation, quietness, revelation, ecstasy, visions and angelic encounters for His name's sake!

Of course, we need to *test the spirits* and confirm every teaching, belief, and practice by the Bible and by the witness of truly godly eldership. But we must remember that there is a fear that comes from Satan, and that where this wrong kind of fear is concerned, *perfect love casts out fear*. We must never allow a "spirit of fear" sent by the enemy to so enslave our hearts just because it sometimes masquerades within the church of God under the guise of "appropriate caution" and "respectability."

Let's summarize some of the basic differences between contemplative life under the authority and protection of the Spirit of God as expressed through the biblical Judeo-Christian ethic and contrast it with the illegal abuses and excesses of advocates of spiritualistic New Age heresies.

2.   Nine Basic Tests

New Testament Christianity	New Age
Who is God?	
Yahweh, the Lord, the Infinite and Personal Creator God	Non-Personal Entity
What is the standard of truth?	
The Judeo-Christian Bible	Evolving, eclectic ancient writings
Who is Jesus Christ	
The Only Begotten Son of God	An enlightened teacher, only one of many ascended Masters
What about Salvation?	
Purchased by the blood of Christ	No such thing, or the acceptance of the enlightenment that you already are god
What is the Focus?	
Christ-centered	Human and self-centered
Where is the source of power?	
Through Christ	Through humanity
What is the source of wisdom?	
God's Divine Wisdom	Human Wisdom
The Next Age	
Ushered in by God	Ushered in by man
The Stance	
Receiving through faith by grace from God	Reaching to become gods

IV.   A WORD OF PERSPECTIVE AND CAUTION

A.   Difficulty in Terms of Description

1.   It is one thing to experience the grace of God's imminent nearness; it is another to be able to communicate it. Sometimes someone who truly has a contemplative experience of God expresses it in a way that upsets the more conservative culture of the church and society. Such a person is often labeled a heretic when he is just expressing himself clumsily.

2.   Mystical language is not necessarily doctrinal, theological language. It is the language of the bedchamber, of love, and hence, hyperbole and exaggeration abound. If a husband says that he adores his wife, it does **not** mean that he regards her as an idol or goddess. He is just trying to express his deep feelings

of love in a language that is powerless to fully convey them - except by excessive hyperbole. But if a people in your area do not understand that kind of language, they may think you are under the influence of "another kind of spirit."

3. As your contemplative inner experience with God deepens, it may become something about which it will be more difficult to speak. It becomes so precious and sublime that it becomes "holy" to you as it is to God.

B. Caution Signals

1. Maintain a balance between the inner life and the outward, active life of servanthood. Contemplative prayer is meant to bring an enabling into our life of service.

2. Spiritual consolation from direct contact with God can be so satisfying that it becomes a trap. You can seek interior prayer for the purpose of escape rather than love. It can become an act of selfish withdrawal rather than of self-surrender.

3. Its beauty is so incomparable, its effect so affirming, its power so transforming that it can lead to spiritual gluttony. Beware of just seeking consolation instead of seeking God Himself.

4. Use common sense, and do not overdo it. Guard the purity of your intentions.

C. So Now, Let's Proceed!

Practice does make perfect. Don't just be an armchair coach or theologian. Step out into the cool quiet stream of contemplative prayer and you will find the great shepherd and lover of our soul - Jesus - who is ready to lead and guide you in your prayer experience.

Reflection Questions
Lesson Five: Contemplative Prayer – What It Is Not

Answers to these questions can be found in the back of the study guide.

Fill in the Blank

1. II Cor. 3:18 – *But we all, with unveiled face _____ as in a mirror the glory of the Lord, are being _____ into the same image from glory to glory.*

2. Psalm 46:10 – *Cease _____ and _____ that I am God; I will be exalted among the nations.*

3. Hebrews 12:2 – *Fixing our eyes on _____, the author and perfecter of faith, who for the joy set before Him, endured the _____ despising the shame...*

Multiple Choice – Choose the best answer from the list below:

A.	You	C.	Sacrifice
B.	Me	D.	Service

4. Gal. 2:20 – *It is no longer I who live but Christ who lives in _____.*

5. Contemplative prayer is meant to bring an enabling into our life of _____.

True or False

6. Contemplative prayer is concerned with divine love between God and man. _____

7. Prayer is not doing something, but being with someone. _____

8. Contemplative prayer is contrary to eastern mysticism and the New Age. _____

Scripture Memorization

9. Write out and memorize Gal. 5: 22-23.

10. What was the primary point you learned from this lesson?

Lesson Six:
Contemplative Prayer: What It Is

I.   CONTEMPLATIVE PRAYER - DEFINING OUR TERMS

A.   From Webster's Dictionary

1. *Contemplate* – 1.) to gaze at intensely. 2.) to think about intensely; to study. 3.) to expect or intend; to meditate; muse.
2. *Muse* – to think or consider deeply; meditate.
3. *Meditate* – to plan; intend; to think deeply; reflect.
4. *Reflect* – 1.) to throw back (light, heat, or sound). 2.) to give back an image (of) mirror. 3.) to bring or come back as a consequence; as reflected glory.
5. *Reflect on (or upon)* – 1.) to contemplate; ponder. 2.) to cast blame or discredit.
6. *Reflective* – 1.) reflecting. 2.) of or produced by reflection. 3.) meditative; thoughtful.

B.   Other Terms Often Used

1. False Self
    This is the "old self" or "old man" (Eph. 4:22-24 (NIV), *You were taught, with regard to your former way of life, to put off your old self, which is being corrupted by its deceitful desires; to be made new in the attitude of your minds; and to put on the new self, created to be like God in true righteousness and holiness.* The "false self" is the ego-centered self-life that holds on to and trusts in "false around" and wrong (untrue), identities wrapped up in whatever possessions or people or power symbols we can lay hold of. The "false self" causes us to cling to other things in order to find happiness, fulfillment, peace, purpose, meaning and life.
2. True Self
    This is the "new self" or "new man" (Col. 3:9,10 NIV). *Do not lie to each other, since you have taken off your old self with its practices and have put on the new self, which is being renewed in knowledge in the image of its Creator.* The true self is the "new man" in Christ that we are, become, and continue to put on. The forming of the "new man," the true self in God, based on the transforming power of Divine love in us, is our participation in the risen life of Christ.

3. Centering – This is a term from (but not exclusive to) Quaker theology and practice. It simply means to "let go of all competing distractions" until we are truly "present with Him." It is the meditative art of quieting, focusing upon the "center" of all life who lives within the heart (spirit/soul) of each believer in Christ Jesus.

4. Recollection – It means to bring together into a unified whole. It is allowing the Holy Spirit to cast light upon our fragmentation so as to bring cleansing and healing into our souls (emotions, remembrances, and thoughts).

5. Union with God – To be made one with our Master and Creator God. It is a work of God upon the heart with two vital preparations from our side of the equation: the love of God and purity of heart.

6. Spiritual Ecstasy – This is derived from the Greek word *ekstasis* which is translated trance in the New Testament. It is an activity initiated by the Holy Spirit where one is "caught up" into a realm of the Spirit so as to receive those things (revelations, visions, experiences) God desires. It is not an activity we undertake, but a work that God does upon us.

7. A Summary – After we have worked our way through all the above, the unintelligible language of contemplatives who are struggling to describe the indescribable, we are reduced to the simple confession of Walter Hilton: Contemplation is "love on fire with devotion."

II. STATEMENTS FROM CHURCH LEADERS [13]

A. From Richard J. Foster – Author of *Prayer: Finding the Heart's True Home*

1. Contemplative Prayer immerses us into the silence of God. How desperately we in the modern world need this wordless baptism! We have become as the early church Father Clement of Alexandria says, "Like old shoes - all worn out except for the tongue. Contemplative Prayer is the one discipline that can free us from our addiction to words.

2. Those who work in the area of spiritual direction always look for signs of a maturing faith before encouraging individuals into Contemplative Prayer. Some of the more common indicators are a continuing hunger for intimacy with God, an ability to forgive others at a great personal cost, a living sense that God alone can satisfy the longings of the human heart, a deep satisfaction in prayer, a realistic assessment of personal abilities and short-comings, a freedom from boasting about spiritual accomplishments, and a demonstrated ability to live out the demands of life patiently and wisely.

3. Contemplative Prayer is a loving attentiveness to God. We are tending to Him who loves us, who is near to us, and who draws us to Himself. In Contemplative Prayer, talk recedes into the background, and feelings come to the foreground.

B. Ammonas – A Desert Father

1. Progress in intimacy with God means progress towards silence. *For God alone my soul waits in silence* (Psalm 62:1). "I have shown you the power of silence, how thoroughly it heals and how fully pleasing it is to God...Know that it is by silence that the saints grew, that is was because of silence that the power of God dwelt in them, because of silence that the mysteries of God were known to them." It is this recreating silence to which we are called in Contemplative Prayer.

C. Bernard of Clairvaux – Twelfth Century Religious and Political Leader in France

1. "We felt that He was present, I remember later that He has been with me; I have sometimes even had a presentiment that He would come; I never felt His coming or leaving." (Bernard's emotional description of God's loving attentiveness during contemplation.)

2. In the Christian life we could find, according to Bernard, three vocations: that of Lazarus, the penitent, that of Martha, the active and devoted servant of the household, and that of Mary, the contemplative. Mary had chosen the "best part" and there was no reason for her to envy Martha or leave her contemplation, unasked, to share in the labors of Martha. In fact, it is unknown for Mary to envy Martha. Contemplation should always be desired and preferred. Activity should be accepted, though never sought. In the end, the completion of the Christian life is found in the union of Martha, Mary and Lazarus in one person.

D. **Francois de Fenelon – Quietist Leader in France in the Late 1600s and Early 1700s**

"Be silent, and listen to God. Let your heart be in such a state of preparation that His Spirit may impress upon you such virtues as will please Him. Let all within you listen to Him. This silence of all outward and earthly affection and of human thoughts within us is essential if we are to hear His voice. This listening prayer does indeed involve a hushing of all outward and earthly affection.

"Return to Prayer and inward fellowship with God no matter what the cost. You have withered your spirit by chasing this wish of yours without knowing if God wanted this for you.

"Don't spend your time making plans that are just cobwebs - a breath of wind will come and blow them away. You have withdrawn from God and now you find that God has withdrawn the sense of His presence from you. Return to Him and give Him everything without reservation. There will be no peace otherwise. Let go of all your plans - God will do what He sees best for you.

"Even if you were to alter your plans through earthly means, God would not bless them. Offer Him your tangled mess and He will turn everything toward His own merciful purpose. The most important thing is to go back to communion with God - even if it seems dry and you are easily distracted."

E. **Thomas Merton – Twentieth Century Writer and Priest**

"Without the spirit of contemplation in all our worship - that is to say without the adoration and love of God above all, for His own sake, because He is God - the liturgy will not nourish a real Christian apostolate based on Christ's love and carried out in the power of the *Pneuma* (Spirit)."

"The most important need in the Christian world today is this inner truth nourished by this Spirit of contemplation: the praise and love of God, the longing for the coming of Christ, the thirst for the manifestation of God's glory, His truth, His justice, His kingdom in the world. These are all characteristically "contemplative" and eschatological aspirations of the Christian heart, and they are the very essence of monastic prayer. Without them our apostolate is more for our own glory rather than the glory of God.

"Without contemplation and interior prayer, the church cannot fulfill her mission to transform and save mankind. Without contemplation, she will be reduced to being the servant of cynical and worldly powers, no matter how hard her faithful may protest that they are fighting for the kingdom of God.

"Without true, deep contemplative aspirations, without a total love for God and an uncompromising thirst for His truth, religion tends in the end to become an opiate."

III. A DESCRIPTION OF CONTEMPLATIVE PRAYER

1. Contemplative Prayer is an exercise of letting go of the control of your own life by leaning on the props of the false self.
2. It is a kind of communion intended to increase our intimacy with God and awareness of His presence.
3. It is a step of submission where we place our being at God's disposal and request His work of purification.
4. In Contemplative Prayer, we are opening ourselves up to the Holy Spirit to get in touch with our true selves and to facilitate an abiding state of union with God.
5. It is an exercise in learning self-surrender. It teaches us to yield, let go and not be possessive.
6. It is a method of exposing and disengaging from the ordinary obstacles to our awareness of God's presence with us. This prayer is not an end, but a beginning.
7. It is being still in order to know God (Psalm 46:10).
8. In Contemplative Prayer, we cultivate the desire to forget ourselves and know God by faith. It is our consent for God's presence and action take over (Col. 3:10).
9. It is a movement beyond conversation, a discipline to foster, that leads us into greater faith, hope, and love.
10. It is an exercise in resting in God. It is not a state of suspension of all activity, but the reductions of many acts to a simple act of saying, "Yes" to God's presence during a time of inner, quiet, devotional prayer.
11. Contemplative Prayer is the trusting and loving faith by which God elevates the human person and purifies the conscious and unconscious obstacles in us that oppose the values of the gospel and the work of the Spirit.
12. It is an activity aimed at fostering the conviction and realization that God lives in us!
13. This is an exercise in purifying our intentions to desire only one thing - God. It is an act of love, a desire not for the experience of God - but for God Himself.

14. Contemplative Prayer is a discipline which facilitates not only living in God's presence but out of God's presence. Its transforming effects cause the divine word to once again be incarnated in human form.

15. Contemplative Prayer is a discipline that enables our developing relationship with Jesus Christ to reach stages of growth in union with God.

IV. GOALS AND BENEFITS OF CONTEMPLATIVE PRAYER [14]
Adapted from Dr. Steve Meeks – Pastor, Calvary Community Church

1. By means of Contemplative Prayer, the Spirit heals the roots of self-centeredness and becomes the source of our conscious activity.

2. This prayer helps us to become aware of the presence of God. Living out of that awareness, we gain strength to meet opposition and contradiction without feeling threatened. The continuing awareness of divine love saves us from the need of human affirmation and recognition. It heals negative feelings we have about ourselves.

3. This form of transforming prayer fosters a different attitude toward one's feelings; it puts them in a different frame of reference. Many of our negative feelings come from a sense of insecurity and the need to build up the empire of self, especially when we feel threatened. But when you are constantly being reaffirmed by God's loving presence, you are no longer afraid to be contradicted or imposed on. Humility will grow as you mature in God's lavish love.

4. This prayer leads us below the conversational level into communion with Him. It basically makes God "more real" to us.

5. As you trust in God and His love for us increases, you are less afraid to have your dark side exposed. We are enabled to "walk in the light as He is in the light and the blood of Jesus cleanses us from all sin." (The truth be known, God always knew the dark side of your character, has loved you all the time, and is now letting you in on His special secret.)

6. The interior silence of Contemplative Prayer brings such a profound cleansing to our whole being that our emotional blocks begin to soften up and our system begins to flush out these poisonous toxins. Bondages may be broken and strongholds destroyed.

7. Although great interior peace may be experienced, this is not the goal. The purpose is not even union with God in a prayer experience. It is to transform us to carry this wholeness with God into the other aspects of everyday life. We are not seeking experiences, but the permanent abiding awareness of being joined to God.

8. Contemplative Prayer will enable you to work for and with others with liberty of spirit because one is no longer seeking one's own ego-centered goals but responding to reality as it is with His divine love.

9. Union with God enables us to handle greater trials. God does not make us like Him in order for Him to merely look at us! He wants us to do something. Let's release the fragrance of Christ wherever we go.

10. Contemplative Prayer teaches us patience, to wait on God, strength for interior silence, and makes us sensitive to the delicate movements of the Spirit in daily life and ministry.

11. Contemplative Prayer illumines the source and strengthens the practice of all other types of devotions. It gets us in touch with the Divine life dwelling in us and thus aiding all spiritual disciplines in becoming relational practices.

12. This divine life is actually going on within us twenty-four hours a day. Much of the time, we do not see it, experience it or release it. We thus live out of the false empire of self, shutting down the flow of God's divine presence and love.

13. Contemplative Prayer aids us in identifying, experiencing, and releasing His life in and through us as we continue to cultivate the wondrous progression of being immersed into His healing love.

14. As Madame Guyon stated, "This is why God sends a fire to the earth. It's to destroy all that is impure in you. Nothing can resist the power of that fire. It consumes everything. His wisdom burns away all the impurities in a man for one purpose - to leave him fit for divine union."

V.   THE PROGRESSIVE STEPS

A.   Recollection – Phase One

1. Letting go of all competing distractions.

2. Focusing not on what has been (guilt, woundedness, etc.) or the future (guidance, words, calling, promises of God not yet fulfilled) but on God in the present tense.

3. *Casting our anxieties* (cares, worries, fears, tensions) *upon Him, for He cares for you.* (I Peter 5:7)

4. While resting, as the Holy Spirit makes Jesus real to you, close everything off. Picture Jesus sitting in a chair across from you, for He is truly present. God created human imagination. Utilizing your imagination in contemplation is appropriate and one of the best uses by which we can deploy it. This is *not* the same as New Age "imagery and imaging" but simply practicing the presence of God.

5. If frustration and distractions attempt to press in on us, do not follow them (trail after them). But rather, just lift them up into the Father and let Him now care for them.

6. Hear Him say, "Peace, be still." Allow this silence to still our noisy hearts.

7. This centeredness does not come easily or quickly. Being aware of this is even a step in the right direction. Experiencing your inability to conquer these distractions is as well another major stride forward.

Romano Guardini notes, "When we try to compose ourselves, unrest redoubles in intensity, not unlike the manner in which at night, when we try to sleep, cares or desires assail us with a force they do not possess during the day. Realize, we are not wasting our time. If at first we achieve no more than the understanding of how much we lack in inner unity, something will have been gained, for in some way we will have made contact with the center which knows no distraction."

B. The Prayer of Quiet – Phase Two [15]

As we grow accustomed to the unifying grace of recollection, we are ushered into a second phase in Contemplative Prayer, what Teresa of Avila calls, "The prayer of quiet."

We have through recollection put away all obstacles of the heart, all distractions of the mind, all vacillations of the will. Divine graces of love and adoration wash over us like ocean waves. At the center of our being we are hushed. There is stillness to be sure, but is a listening stillness. Something deep inside us has been awakened and brought to attention. Our spirit is on tiptoe - alert and listening. There now comes an inward steady gaze of the heart sometimes called beholding the Lord. Now we bask in the warmth of His dear embrace.

As we wait before God, graciously we are given a teachable spirit. Of course, our goal is to bring this contentment into everyday expressions of life. This does not come to us quickly. However, as we experience more and more of an inward attentiveness to His divine whisper, we will carry His presence through our day. Just as smoke is absorbed into our clothing and we carry its smell with us, so the aroma of God's presence is seeping into our being and we will likewise carry His gracious fragrance wherever we go.

(Material concerning handling noise, distractions, etc. is developed in the series, *Quieting Our Souls Before the Lord*. More material is developed on the interior peace in the next lesson of "The Center of Quiet.")

C. Spiritual Ecstasy – Phase Three

The final step into Contemplative Prayer is spiritual ecstasy. This is not an activity or undertaking, but a work that God does upon us. Ecstasy is Contemplative Prayer taken to "the nth degree." Even the recognized authorities in the contemplative life found it to be a fleeting experience rather than a staple diet.

1. Theodore Brakel – Dutch Pietist in the Seventeenth Century

"I was transported into such a state of joy and my thoughts were so drawn upward that, seeing God with the eyes of my soul, I felt God's being and at the same time I was so filled with joy, peace, and sweetness that I cannot express it."

2. Saint Augustine of Hippo – Fourth Century "Doctor" of the Latin Church

Augustine turned his back on God during his early adult years. But his mother, Monica, who herself came to be known as "Santa Monica" prayed faithfully and earnestly for many years for her son until he finally came into the kingdom of God. They had an experience on the Tiber River at the city of Ostia.

They were gazing out a window with deep yearning for God when "With the mouth of our heart we panted for the heavenly streams of Your fountain, the fountain of life." As they were talking, however, words failed them and they were raised "higher and step by step passed over all material things, even the heaven itself from which sun and moon and stars shine down upon the earth. And still we went upward, meditating and speaking and looking with wonder at Your works. We came to our own souls, and we went beyond our souls to reach that region of never-failing plenty where 'Thou feedest Israel' forever with the food of truth.' We sighed and left captured there the first fruits of our spirits and made our way back to the sound of our voices, where a word has both beginning and end."

(The subject of trances is covered in detail in the study guide: *Understanding Supernatural Encounters*.)

VI.   PRAYER IN THE PRESENT TENSE

A.   A Poem of Reflection about the Present Tense God

I was regretting the past and fearing the future.
Suddenly, my Lord was speaking:

"My name is I AM." He paused.
I waited. He continued,
"When you live in the past,
With its mistakes and regrets,
It is hard. I am not there.
My name is not I WAS.

"When you live in the future,
With its problems and fears,
It is hard. I am not there.
My name is not I WILL BE.

"When you live in this moment,
It is not hard. I AM here.
My name is I AM."

by Helen Mallicoat

B.   Getting Comfortable with God

Many of us struggle with resting and waiting in God's presence, perhaps because we think He has something against us or we are just too busy. While He calls us into change, He does so by wrapping His arms of love all around us. This takes time before you learn to trust that the best place to be is in your Father's arms. But this will happen. Why? Because He is more committed to the journey than you are! So come on in and commune with Him. He is waiting for you.

C.   Closing Prayer

"Lord, lead me into these ancient paths, get fresh and vital for today. Teach me Your ways. Silence my fears. Bring me into greater unity with Your Spirit that I might release Your fragrance wherever I go. Amen."

Reflection Questions
Lesson Six: Contemplative Prayer – What It Is

Answers to these questions can be found in the back of the study guide.

1. Questions to Ponder

    a. Am I becoming less afraid of being known and owned by God? Write your thoughts down as you commune with Him.

    b. Is prayer developing in me as a welcomed discipline? Express your desires and failures.

    c. Am I learning to move beyond personal offense and freely forgive those who hurt me?

2. Reflection on Psalm 42:1-2 – *As a deer pants for streams of water so my soul pants for you, O God. My soul thirsts for God, for the living God.* Muse upon this verse and ponder it. Now let the Holy Spirit reveal this to you. Wait, and look with your heart. See the panting deer approaching the brook of living waters.

    a. What are the waters of which your soul thirsts?

    b. What is the name of the river from which you need to drink?

    c. What is the stream from which you presently drink?

    d. Are the waters clear or polluted? Let the Lord now create in you a greater thirst for Him. Now let Him quench that thirst.

Lesson Seven:
The Center of Quiet

I. FIVE INGREDIENTS OF THE CONTEMPLATIVE/MEDITATIVE STATE

A. Biblical Exhortation Concerning Physical Calm

1. Hebrews 4:9-11
There remains therefore a Sabbath rest for the people of God. For the one who has entered His rest has himself also rested from his works, as God did from His. Let us therefore be diligent to enter that rest, lest anyone fall through following the same example of disobedience.

2. Hebrews 3:18,19
And to whom did He swear that they should not enter His rest, but to those who were disobedient? And so we see that they were not able to enter because of unbelief.

B. Biblical Exhortation Concerning Focused Attention

1. Hebrews 12:1,2
Let us...lay aside every encumbrance, and...sin which so easily entangles us, and let us run...fixing our eyes on Jesus, the author and perfecter of faith.

2. John 5:19
Truly, truly I say to you, the Son can do nothing of Himself, unless it is something He sees the Father doing; for whatever the Father does, these things the So does in like manner.

C. Biblical Exhortation Concerning Letting Go

1. Psalm 46:10
Cease striving (let go, relax) *and know that I am God.*

2. Philippians 4:6,7
Be anxious for nothing, but in everything by prayer and supplication with thanksgiving let your requests be made known to God. And the peace of God, which surpasses all comprehension, shall guard your hearts and your minds in Christ Jesus.

D. Biblical Exhortation Concerning Receptivity

1. John 15:45
   Abide in Me, and I in you, as the branch cannot bear fruit of itself, unless it abides in the vine, so neither can you, unless you abide in Me. I am the vine, you are the branches; he who abides in Me and I in him, he bears much fruit; for apart from Me, you can do nothing.
2. Samuel 3:3-4
   And the lamp of God had not yet gone out, and Samuel was lying down in the temple of the Lord where the ark of God was, that the Lord called Samuel; and he said, "Here I am".

E. Biblical Exhortation Concerning Spontaneous Flow

1. John 7:38, 39
   He who believes in Me, as the Scripture said, "From his innermost being shall flow rivers of living water." But this He spoke of the Spirit, whom those who believed in him were to receive."
2. Revelation 4:1-2
   After these things I looked, and behold, a door standing open in heaven, and the first voice which I heard, like the sound of a trumpet speaking with me, said, "Come up here, and I will show you what must take place after these things". Immediately I was in the Spirit; and behold, a throne was standing in heaven and one sitting on the throne.

II. PRAYER IS BECOMING A FRIEND

A. Five Stages

Stage 1 – Casual
   I speak of the world outside me (sports, weather).
Stage 2 – Beginning Trust
   I speak of what I think and feel.
Stage 3 – Deep Trust
   I share my dreams, mistakes, and frustrations.
Stage 4 – Intimacy
   sit quietly with my Friend, experiencing a Presence beyond words.
Stage 5 – Union
   I become one with that person; speaking, feeling and acting with His reactions.

B. I Call You Friends

1. John 15:15
   No longer do I call you servants, I now call you friends.
2. Prayer is two lovers sharing intimate communion together. It is not as much "doing something" as it is "being with someone."
3. If ultimately prayer is desire expressed, in all our intercessions, petitioning, pleading, and reminding, let's make sure that we continue to "hold onto His hand upward" as we "reach out in faith outward." Let's let our desire be expressed (prayer) for a greater friendship with Him.

III. THE PRAYER OF REST

There are three well-established practices designed to lead us into the Prayer of Rest. Let's look briefly at them:

A. Solitude - Step One

1. Mark 1:35 RSV
   In the morning, a great while before day, He rose and went out to a lonely place.
2. Matthew 6:6 NAS
   But you, when you pray, go into your inner room, and when you have shut your door, pray to your Father who is in secret, and your Father who sees in secret will repay you.
3. **Dallas Willard – *The Spirit of the Disciplines*** [16]
   "We must re-emphasize, the 'desert' or 'closet' is the primary place of strength for the beginner, as it was for Christ and for Paul. They show us by their example what we must do. In stark aloneness, it is possible to have silence, to be still, and to know that Jehovah, indeed, is God (Psa. 46:10), to set the Lord before our minds with sufficient intensity and duration that we stay centered upon Him – our hearts fixed, established in trust (Psa. 112:7,8) even when back in the office, shop, or home."
4. **David Runcorn – *A Center of Quiet*** [17]
   "He (Jesus) made silence and solitude His special companions. Whatever the demands upon Him, He always found a time and a place to hide away and be alone. His hectic teaching and ministering was constantly punctuated by these times of withdrawal. Before all the most important events in His life we find Him preparing by getting alone. His ministry began in the wilderness (Mt. 4:1-11). He chose His disciples after a whole night alone in prayer (Lk 6:12). When John the Baptist died, Jesus spent time alone (Mt. 14:13). Before the glory of the transfiguration and darkness of the cross, we find Him alone in

prayer (Mt. 17:1-9; 26:36-46). In those lonely places, the deep springs of the Spirit's life revived Him, the Father's will strengthened Him and the Father's love inspired Him.

"He taught the disciples to do the same. After one particular busy time of ministry and teaching he said, *'Come with me by yourselves to a quiet place and get some rest.' So they went away by themselves in a boat to a lonely place* (Mk. 6:31, 32)."

5.   **Francois de Fenelon – *The Seeking Heart*** [18]
"If you give up all those things that provoke your curiosity and set your mind spinning, you will have more than enough time to spend with God and to attend to your business.

"Living your life prayerfully will make you clear-headed and calm, no matter what happens. Your self-nature is overactive, impulsive and always striving for something just outside your reach.

"But God, working within your spirit, produces a calm and faithful heart that the world cannot touch. I really want you to take an adequate amount of time to spend with God so that you might refresh your spirit. All your busyness surely drains you. Jesus took His disciples aside to be alone, and interrupted their most urgent business. Sometimes He would even leave people who had come from afar to see Him in order to come to His Father. I suggest you do the same. It is not enough to give out - you must learn to receive from God, too."

B.   **Silence – Step Two**
A second time-honored practice is silence, or stilling of what others called "creaturely activity."

1.   **Dallas Willard – Author and Professor** [19]
"Hearing is said to be the last of our senses to go at death. Sound always strikes deeply and disturbingly into our souls. So, for the sake of our souls, we must seek times to leave our television, radio, tape players, and telephones off. We should close off street noises as much as possible. We should try to find how quiet we can make our world by making whatever arrangements are necessary."

2.   **David Runcorn – Anglican Priest** [20]
"If you have a magazine or newspaper handy, try reading an article without using the punctuation marks. It doesn't make much sense does it? It all becomes a hectic string of words. The meaning is lost. It lacks direction. The purpose of punctuation in a piece of writing is to guide the reader into the true meaning of the words and phrases; through it we understand. Punctuation

also gives life and purpose to the words. Next time you see your favorite actor or actress on television, notice how cleverly they use timing – pauses and spaces – to give the words their meaning and power.

"Punctuation is a helpful way of thinking about Jesus' relation with silence and solitude. His times alone were the commas, pauses and full stops in the story of His life. They gave the rest of His life its structure, direction and balance. His words and His works were born out of those hours of silent waiting upon God."

3. **Richard J. Foster – Author and Teacher** [21]

"This agitated creaturely activity hinders the work of God in us. In silence, we still every motion that is not rooted in God. We become quiet, hushed, motionless, until we are finally centered. We let go of all distractions until we are driven into the core. We allow God to reshuffle our priorities and eliminate unnecessary froth. This means not so much a silence of words as a silence of our grasping, manipulative control of people and situations. It means standing firm against our codependency, drives to control everyone and fix everything."

C.   Recollection – Step Three [22]

1.   What Is It?
This means coming into tranquility of mind, heart, and spirit. Isaiah 30:15 tells us, *In repentance and rest you shall be saved, in quietness and trust is your strength.* We have somewhat covered "recollection" in the lesson, "Contemplative Prayer – What It Is".

2.   The Parable of the Wounded Bird
What would happen if I close my hands completely? It would be crushed and die. What would happen if I open my hands completely? It would try to fly away, and it will fall and die. The right place, the right balance, then, is my cupped hands - neither totally open nor totally closed. It is the space where growth and healing can take place. So is the prayer of rest.

IV. TOWARDS A GREATER UNION

A. What is the Goal?

1. Juliana of Norwich – 14th Century English Mystic
    The whole reason why we pray is to be united into the vision and contemplation of Him to whom we pray.

2. Bonaventure – Follower of Saint Francis
    Our final goal is union with God, which is a pure relationship where we see nothing.

3. Madame Guyon – *Experiencing The Depths of Jesus Christ*
    "As you come into the deeper level of knowing the Lord, you will eventually come to discover a principle I will call the law of central tendency.

    "What do you mean by the law of central tendency? As you continue holding your soul deep in your inward parts, you will discover that God has a magnetic attracting quality. Your God is like a magnet! The Lord naturally draws you more and more toward Himself.

    "We come now to the ultimate stage of Christian experience. **Divine Union**. This cannot be brought about merely by your own experience. Meditation will not bring Divine Union; neither will love, nor worship, nor your direction, nor your sacrifice... Eventually it will take an **Act of God** to make Union a reality.

    "Then let us agree on this: There is Divine Union, and there is a way. The way has a beginning, a progress, and a point of arrival. Furthermore, the closer you come to the consummation, the more you put aside the things that helped you get started.

    "Of course, there is also a middle, for you cannot go from a beginning to an end without there being an intermediate space. But if the end is good and holy and necessary, and if the entrance is also good, you can be sure the journey between those two points is also good!"

V.   THERE IS A QUIET PLACE

A.   In the Midst of Every Storm

In the midst of every storm, there is the center (eye) of quiet. As it is in the natural, so it is in the Spirit. There is a refuge to which we can turn. Just as there is a progression in Moses' Tabernacle to the Most Holy Place, so there is a progression to the place of quiet communion within the kingdom of God within each believer. There is a place where God dwells and in Him there is perfect peace.

B.   A Prayer for Quiet [23]

From *Prayers from the Heart* by Richard J. Foster

"I have, O Lord, a noisy heart. And entering outward silence doesn't stop the inner clamor. In fact, it seems only to make it worse. When I am full of activity, the internal noise is only a distant rumble; but when I get still, the rumble amplifies itself. And it is not like the majestic sound of a symphony rising to a grand crescendo; rather it is the deafening din of clashing pots and changing pans. What a racket! Worst of all, I feel helpless to hush the interior pandemonium.

"Dear Lord Jesus, once You spoke peace to the wind and waves. Speak Your shalom over my heart. I wait silently...patiently. I receive into the very core of my being Your loving command, 'Peace, be still.' Amen."

C.   A Contemporary Song

There is a Quiet Place [24]
by Ralph Carmichael

There is a Quiet Place
Far from the rapid pace
Where God can soothe your troubled mind.

Whether a mountain tall
Or a river small
New strength and courage there I find.

Then from this Quiet Place
Go prepared to face
A new day with love for all mankind.

Reflective Questions
Lesson Seven: The Center of Quiet

Answers to these questions can be found in the back of the study guide.

1. Read Psalm 62. Read it slowly. What pictures come to mind as you read?

   Now read it again. Read it from the heart. Read it with pauses and waiting. Let faith, hope and love arise in your heart realizing "power belongs to God." Write down some of your thoughts.

2. Try writing your own personal psalm, using parts of your world and environment to express your longing and feelings.

3. Now express in prayer, your own longings for the Center of Quiet to be developed in your life. Tell the Lord your intimate longings and desires into which you want to enter.

Lesson Eight:
Journey into the Interior Castle

I.   **AN OVERVIEW OF THE BOOK - *INTERIOR CASTLE*** [25]

The following is a synopsis of the visionary experiences of the founder of the Carmelites, Saint Teresa of Avila who lived in Spain during the 16th century. It portrays progressive rooms we enter in while on our intimate pursuit of our union with God.

A.   The Beginning

I began to think of the soul as if it were a castle made of a single diamond or of very clear crystal, in which there are many rooms, just as in Heaven there are many mansions.

These mansions are not "arranged in a row one behind another" but variously - "some above, others below, others at each side; and in the center and midst of them all is the chief mansion, where the most secret things pass between God and the soul."

The figure is used to describe the whole course of the mystical life - the soul's progress from the First Mansions to the Seventh and its transformation from an imperfect and sinful creature into the Bride of the Spiritual Marriage. The door by which it first enters the castle is prayer and meditation. Once inside, "it must be allowed to roam through these mansions" and "not be compelled to remain for a long time in one single room." But it must also cultivate self-knowledge and "begin by entering the room where humility is acquired rather than by flying off to the other rooms. For that is the way to progress."

B.   First Mansions

This chapter begins with a meditation on the excellence and dignity of the human soul, made as it is in the image and likeness of God: the author laments that more pains are not taken to perfect it. The souls in the First Mansions are in a state of grace, but are still very much in love with the venomous creatures outside the castle - that is, with occasions of sin - and need a long and searching discipline before they can make any progress. So they stay for a long time in the Mansions of Humility, in which, since the heat and light from within reach them only in a faint and diffused form, all is cold and dim.

C.   Second Mansions

But all the time the soul is anxious to penetrate farther into the castle, so it seeks every opportunity of advancement - sermons, edifying conversations, good company and so on. It is doing its utmost to put its desires into practice: these are the Mansions of the Practice of Prayer. It is not yet completely secure from the attacks of the poisonous reptiles, which infest the courtyard of the castle, but is powers of resistance are increasing. There is more warmth and light here than in the First Mansions.

D. Third Mansions

The description of these Mansions of Exemplary Life begins with stern exhortations on the dangers of trusting to one's own strength and to the virtues one has already acquired, which must still of necessity be very weak. Yet, although the soul which reaches the Third Mansions may still fall back, it has attained a high standard of virtue. Controlled by discipline and penance and disposed to performing acts of charity toward others, it has acquired prudence and discretion and orders its life well. Its limitations are those of vision: it has not yet experienced to the full the inspiring force of love. It has not made a full self-oblation, a total self-surrender. Its love is still governed by reason, and so its progress is slow. It suffers from aridity, and is given only occasional glimpses into the Mansions beyond.

E. Fourth Mansions

Here the supernatural element of the mystical life first enters: that is to say, is no longer by its own efforts that the soul is acquiring what it gains. Henceforward the soul's part will become increasing less and God's part increasingly greater. The graces of the Fourth Mansions, referred to as "spiritual consolations", are identified with the Prayer of Quiet, or the Second Water, the *Life*. The soul is like a fountain built near its source and the water of life flows into it, not through an aqueduct, but directly from the spring. Its love is now free from servile fear: it has broken all the bonds which previously hindered its progress; it shrinks from no trials and attaches no importance to anything to do with the world. It can pass rapidly from ordinary to infused prayer and back again. It has not yet, however, received the highest gifts of the Spirit and relapses are still possible.

F. Fifth Mansions

This is the state described elsewhere as the Third Water, the Spiritual Betrothal, and the Prayer of Union – that is, incipient Union. It marks a new degree of infused contemplation and a very high one. By means of the most celebrated of all her metaphors, that of the silkworm, St. Teresa explains how far the soul can prepare itself to receive what is essentially a gift from God. She also describes the psychological conditions of this state, in which, for the first time, the faculties of the soul are "asleep." It is of short duration, but while it lasts, the soul is completely possessed by God.

G.   **Sixth Mansions**
In the Fifth Mansions the soul is, as it were, betrothed to its future spouse; in the Sixth, Lover and Beloved see each other for long periods at a time, and as they grow in intimacy the soul receives increasing favors, together with increasing afflictions. The afflictions which give the description of these Mansions its characteristic color are dealt with in some detail. They may be purely exterior – bodily sickness, misrepresentation, backbiting and persecution; undeserved praise; inexperienced, timid or over-scrupulous spiritual direction. Or they may come partly or wholly from within – and the depression which can afflict the soul in the Sixth Mansions, says St. Teresa is comparable only with the tortures of hell. Yet it has no desire to be freed from them except by entering the innermost Mansions of all.

H.   **Seventh Mansions**
Here at last, the soul reaches the Spiritual Marriage. Here dwells the King - "it may be called another Heaven": the two lighted candles join and become one, the falling rain becomes merged in the river. There is complete transformation, ineffable and perfect peace; no higher state is conceivable, save that of the Beatific Vision in the life to come.

II.   CURRENT DAY REVELATORY EXPERIENCE

A dear intercessory friend, Donna Spencer, had the privilege of receiving the following encounters with her Lord. The following is her testimony:

A.   **Dream – March 21, 1996**
"I am falling in love with a wonderful man who is my friend. He is sitting in a large overstuffed chair. He scoots over to the right and pats the seat next to him and says, "Come here." I sit down and we are very close, shoulder-to-shoulder. He begins to whisper in my ear telling me how much he loves me and I can feel his breath on my cheek as he speaks. I felt overwhelmed by his love. We kiss for the first time gently and tenderly and then he kisses me deeply and passionately. I am filled with a powerful array of emotions. As his love flooded over me, my whole being responded with love in return."

B.   **Dream/Visitation – March 22, 1996**
The above short dream prefaced the following experience.

"It was dark and I and some others were running away from some evil and we climbed a tree – then I met the man I love...the Lord.

"There was a mansion (meaning from *Strong's* is a staying, the act of or the place of one's residence, to dwell or abide. John 14:2). My love took me in and went to some stairs leading to the top floor. There was a woman watching Him take me upstairs and I knew she had not been taken there before. There were many rooms, each with unique and unusual decor – gifts, hand-craved, hand-painted molding and beautiful things to see.

"I was astounded and in awe as I went from room to room exclaiming like a child 'Oh! Look at this! Ooh...' He was as delighted in my delight as I was in all of it and in Him. Suddenly as I looked at Him, His love pierced me so deeply I could hardly stand it! Everything within me came alive in response to His love. No words or adjectives could tell of what I felt.

"Next, we were sitting on a set of front steps. He began to cry, 'Oh where is my Sasha, she's been gone so long. Where is my Sasha?' As deeply as I had felt His love I could feel His deep pain. I hugged Him and wiped His tears and kissed his cheek, the pain was so great.

"I saw in a vision (as He was crying) a young girl with long black hair, and I knew this to be Sasha. (Sasha is a name of endearment and intimacy, which comes from the name Alexander which means 'helper, defender, protecter of mankind'). When He stopped crying He turned and said, 'Let's play a game,' and I noticed how His eyes were crystal clear and bright. I said, 'Okay.'

"We went into the house to a lower level room and there was a low table with a castle on it and playing pieces. The castle was an indescribable white/crystallized substance. There was someone sitting at the head of the table (the Father, I think). I was sitting to His right and Jesus was sitting on my right. I picked two small pieces and we began to have fun (we were playing a kind of mock battle with our pieces). I wasn't even sure how to play and kept asking how to play.

"Suddenly, a woman with long black hair came to Jesus' right and the Father said, 'Give her the 'daughter' piece,' and I knew the piece she had was stronger than my pieces. She played for a short while (my impression of her actions while she played was that she was flirtatious and intimate on a superficial level) then leaned over Him and became somewhat familiar, then began to leave. He reached His right hand out to her and as only their fingertips touched, I could feel His pain and I couldn't understand what was happening.

"I couldn't understand how she could leave Him because His love was so great. I said, 'I will love you with all my heart with the deepest part of my being. I will give you my life and do all I can for you - but how can you love her (since she left Him) and love me too?' Still looking at her He said, 'I *have* loved her but she went away and found other things and hasn't come back to Me.' He released her hand and leaned upon my shoulder.

"The Father said I could choose five game pieces, I chose five very unusual pieces but one in particular struck me. It was silver with a ball in the center filled with a red substance, (silver symbolizes redemption, and red the blood of Jesus). I sensed an authority come upon me knowing that I am His bride and that He is my beloved.

"The woman who had been watching saw this and said she couldn't stay now since I picked up those pieces. (I knew this was her choice to leave, she could have chosen to stay with Him).

"Next, I carried a piece of my flesh wrapped in a white cloth. Following behind me on either side were two companions. I was walking towards a furnace through a courtyard filled with furniture, etc. As I very ceremoniously placed my offering into the fire, I immediately knew it wasn't sufficient. My companions were gone and everything began to change. I was surrounded by hundreds of manifested demons and great darkness. The furniture was walking and the walls became huge black demons. I then knew there must be a sacrifice of all consuming fire and I lay down in front of the furnace. Pure holy fire came out of the furnace over me and I was transformed. It didn't hurt and I wasn't afraid. I was surprised to learn I wasn't dead but completely changed. The darkness and demons fled.

"The Bridal Chamber. To the side, I saw a small room with a very narrow bed and an old plaid cover on it. There was a hole in the slanted ceiling over the bed and plaster had fallen everywhere. I knew that whoever fixed this room didn't really love Him. (Could this narrow bed represent the Law?) As He took my hand and led me back to the larger room, I noticed the Father was there watching us. Then I saw a huge bed covered in the finest fabric of ivory and soft rose colors. It was so peaceful and inviting, so pure and lovely. I saw a double-paned window of etched glass. I opened the latch and looked out. It was so beautiful! There were stars like diamonds and brilliant light everywhere...I was awed. I turned back and saw Him watching me. I went to Him and we embraced. I was once again so filled with His love that I was overcome."

III. OUR FATHER'S HOUSE

A. Primary Scriptures – John 14:1-8

"Do not let your hearts be troubled. Trust in God; trust also in Me. In My Father's house are many rooms; if it were not so, I would have told you. I am going there to prepare a place for you. And if I go and prepare a place for you, I will come back and take you to be with Me that you also may be where I am. You know the way to the place where I am going." Thomas said to him, "Lord, we don't know where You are going, so how can we know the way?" Jesus answered, "I am the way and the truth and the life. No one comes to the Father except through Me. If you really knew Me, you would know my Father as well. From now on, you do know Him and have seen Him." Philip said, "Lord, show us the Father and that will be enough for us."

B. Let Him Fill Each Room

As we take the path less traveled into the "Inward Journey" we find it is a joyful pathway. We are the temple of God – Our Father's House. We are the dwelling place of God by the Holy Spirit. Let Him cleanse each room in His mansion and take up residence within. Ask Him to inhabit and fill each room of this castle and take possession of you! It will be a journey that will last a lifetime and one that is full of life abundantly.

Reflection Questions
Lesson Eight: Journey into the Interior Castle

Answers to these questions can be found in the back of the study guide.

1. Read John 14:1-3. Read this verse slowly. What pictures come to mind as you read it?

   "Do not let your hearts be troubled. Trust in God; trust also in Me. In My Father's house are many rooms; if it were not so, I would have told you. I am going there to prepare a place for you. And if I go and prepare a place for you, I will come back and take you to be with Me that you also may be where I am".

2. Now read it again. Read it slowly from the heart. Read it with pauses and waiting. Let the reality come to you that you are the "Father's House". Now write out some additional impressions that come to you.

3. Read I Corinthians 3:17 and II Corinthians 6:16. Compare these passages. What do these passages have in common?

   Are there rooms in your temple that need to be cleansed? Ask God the Father to come now and cleanse each room by the blood of Jesus.

4. Now in closing, express in prayer your heart's longing for each room to be inhabited and filled with the presence of Jesus. Slowly do this. Write out your experience as He comes to fill each room.

Section Three

Cultivating Spiritual Disciplines

Lesson Nine:
Christian Meditative Prayer

I. TAKING A FRESH LOOK

Once again, I feel the need to be a Holy Spirit archaeologist and like the "Indiana Jones" of fabled movies, I need to take a little whiskbroom and dust off some misconceptions off these Lost Treasures of the Body of Christ. So I invite you to go with me on a journey to rediscover one of the arts of spiritual disciplines called Meditation, or, Christian Meditative Prayer. Let's consider some definitions of our subject from a variety of trusted voices.

A. Toward a Working Definition

1. Elmer L. Towns – Vice President of Liberty University
"Christian Meditation is not about what methods you use, nor is it about what position you assume, nor is it about what you chant or how you focus. Christian Meditation is about God, it is meditation that will change your life because you focus on God – and when you experience God, it is God who changes you." [26]

2. Richard J. Foster – Author and Quaker Teacher
"Throughout history all the devotional masters have viewed the meditative *scripturarum*, the meditation upon Scripture, as the central reference point by which all other forms of meditation are kept in proper perspective. In Meditative Prayer the Bible ceases to be a quotation dictionary and become instead 'wonderful words of life' that lead us to the word of Life. It differs even from the study of Scripture. Whereas, the study of Scripture centers on exegesis, the meditation upon Scriptures centers on internalizing and personalizing the passage. The written Word becomes a living word addressed to us." [27]

3. Peter Toon – Author of *Meditating as a Christian*
"Meditation is…Thinking about, reflecting upon, considering, taking to heart, reading slowly and carefully, prayerfully taking in, and humbly receiving into mind, heart and will that which God has revealed. For Christian meditating…is being guided and inspired by the indwelling Spirit of Christ in the consideration of God's revelation."' [28]

4. Dietrich Bonheoffer – German Author of *The Way to Freedom*
"Just as you do not analyze the assets of someone you love, but accept them as they are said to you, then accept the word of Scripture and ponder it in your heart, as Mary did. That is all. That is meditation." [29]

5. Dr. Sam Storms – Author and Founder of Enjoying God Ministries
    "Meditation, then, is being attentive to God. It is a conscious, continuous engagement of the mind with God. This renewing of the mind (Rom. 12:1-2) is part of the process by which the Word of God penetrates the soul and spirit with the light of illumination and the power of transformation." [30]

6. Tricia McCary Rhodes – Author of *The Soul at Rest*
    "In meditative prayer the Bible is not a rulebook, a history lesson, or a treatise to be dissected and analyzed. We come to its author with our hearts open and our desire for Him. We can hide God's Word in our hearts through meditative prayer. Seeking God's face, we want to understand the person who wrote these powerful words. Our hearts are the soil in which the word is planted. Every part of our being joins together to nourish the seeds of truth until they sprout and bring life to our soul." [31]

7. Dr. Siang-Yang Tan – Author of *Disciplines of the Holy Spirit*
    "Meditation is pondering over scripture verses or passages in such a way that the written Word of God becomes a living word of God applied to our hearts by the Holy Spirit. The two primary words for meditation in the Bible mean 'to murmur or mutter' and 'to speak to one's self.' Meditation is a process of thinking through language that takes place in the heart or inner life. The truth being meditated upon moves from the mouth (murmuring), to the mind (reflective thinking), and finally to the heart (outer action). The person meditating seeks to understand how to relate Bible truth to life." [32]

8. Pat Gastineau – Prayer Leader of Word of Love Ministries
    "Since meditation is mainly for the mind and the will, any meditation that is centered on Christ will hold the mind in place of loving attention toward God. Meditation can cause the mind to hold ideas and thoughts. As one centers his attention on certain aspects of God, the mind is being trained to focus for periods of time. Meditation brings discipline and therefore is one of the answers for unruly minds that tend to run loose. The Scriptures refer to the saving of the soul – the mind must be reprogrammed to think correctly. Meditation will aid in producing a sound mind, one that is sane and sober." [33]

B.   Some Analogies to Help Our Understanding

1.   Richard J. Foster – *Prayer: Finding the Heart's True Home*
"Have you ever watched a cow chew its cud? This unassuming animal will fill its stomach with grass and other food. Then it settles down quietly and, through a process of regurgitation, reworks what it has received, slowly moving its mouth in the process. In this way it is able to fully assimilate what it has previously consumed, which is then transformed into rich, creamy milk. So it is with meditative prayer. The truth being mediated upon passes from the mouth into the mind and down into the heart, where through quiet rumination – regurgitation, if you will – it produces in the person praying, a loving, faith-filled response."[34]

2.   Donald S. Whitney – *Spiritual Disciplines for the Christian Life*
"A simple analogy would be a cup of tea. You are the cup of hot water and the intake of Scripture is represented by the tea bag. Hearing God's Word is like one dip of the tea bag into the cup. Some of the tea's flavor is absorbed by the water, but not as much as would occur with a more thorough soaking of the bag. In this analogy, reading, studying, and memorizing God's Word are represented by additional plunges of the tea bag into the cup. The more frequently the tea enters the water, the more effect it has. Meditation, however, is like immersing the bag completely and letting it steep until all of the rich tea flavor has been extracted and the hot water is thoroughly tinctured reddish brown." [35]

3.   Dr. Siang-Yang Tan – *Disciplines of the Holy Spirit*
"In meditation, we seek to enter into the Scripture and live in it. We stand in the shoes of the disciples, alongside the Pharisees, in the kitchen with Martha, at the feet of Jesus with Mary. As St. Ignatius encourages us to do, we let all of our senses come into play. We see the friends lowering the paralytic through the roof. We smell the salt sea, feel the cool breeze on our face, and hear the lapping of waves along the shore of Galilee. We taste the bread multiplied by Jesus' hands as we sit among the crowd. As the Spirit works, we take time to meet Jesus in each passage, to have lunch with Him, to address Him and to be addressed by Him, to touch the hem of His garment." [36]

II. TEN WAYS TO PRACTICE CHRISTIAN MEDITATION

The Lord is truly revealing fresh insights into these ancient truths. Books have been mentors in my journey. A recent gold mine I have been excavating in is the book *Christian Meditation for Spiritual Breakthrough* by Elmer L. Towns. The following points come from the inspiration of his practical yet classical work. [37]

A. The David Model: Considering God's Creation and Might

1. From the Life of David
    Imagine as the shepherd boy David spent many nights under the stars; looking, gazing, pondering, musing on creation and God the Creator. Creation is where most all of us first encounter God. *The heavens declare the glory of God and the firmament shows His handwork* (Ps. 19). Before people first read about God in the Scriptures, they tend to learn about our heavenly Father through nature. Consider the rainbow – a sign of God's covenant after the great flood (Gen. 9:13). Study the David Model to meditate on the splendor and majesty of God.
2. Scripture Passages on God's Majesty
    a) Job 37:1-24
    b) Psalms 8:1-8
    c) Psalm 19:1-4
    d) Psalm 29:1-11
    e) Psalm 39:1-13
    f) Psalm 90:1-17
    g) Isaiah 40:1-31
    h) Isaiah 44:1-45:25

B. The Mary Model: Pondering the Person of Jesus

1. From Mary – The Mother of Jesus
    Can you begin to imagine what Mary pondered on? Just think – the Son of God growing inside of you. You feel His heart beat; you feel His foot move; you bring Him to birth! Truly, one of closest people ever to Jesus was His Mother Mary. *Mary kept all these things and pondered them in her heart.* (Luke 2:19). She knew Him better than anyone, yet just like us, she wanted to know Him still better. Mary becomes our example of what it means to really know Christ – to come into intimacy with the lover of our soul. Let's join in her model of meditating on the person of Christ Jesus.
2. Scripture Passages on the Person of Jesus
    a) Matthew 1:18 – 2:23
    b) Matthew 3:13 – 4:11

c)   Matthew 9:35 – 10:7
d)   Matthew 16:13 – 17:13
e)   Luke 2:42 – 52
f)   Luke 24:1-53
g)   John 1:1-18
h)   John 2:1-12
i)   John 13:1-35
j)   John 19:1-42
k)   Philippians 2:2-12
l)   Hebrews 5:5-14
m)   Revelation 1:9-20
n)   Revelation 19:11-16

C. The Saint John Model: Thinking about the Cross

1.   From the Life of John the Beloved
When you consider the St. John Model of meditation you center your focus on the finished work of the cross of Jesus. John was the only one of the 12 disciples to stand at the foot of the cross and actually witness the death of our Savior. It changed John. It will change you too. You too will boast only in the great immense love of God. *Behold what manner of love the Father has bestowed on us, that we should be called children of God.* Let's follow John's example and always keep the love of God demonstrated through the cross of Christ ever before us.

2.   Scripture Passages on the Cross
a)   Isaiah 53:1-12
b)   John 19:16-37
c)   Acts 4:10-12
d)   Romans 3:21-26
e)   I Corinthians 11:23,24
f)   Ephesians 1:7; 2:13-18
g)   Colossians 1:14; 2:9-15
h)   Hebrews 9:11-28
i)   I Peter 1:18-23

D. The Joshua Model: Focusing on Biblical Principles

1.   From the Life Joshua, the Successor of Moses
Those who follow the Joshua Model of meditation muse on the promises and principles of God's Word to bring them God's success. *This book of the Law shall not depart from your mouth, but you shall meditate in it day and night, that you may observe to do according to all that is written in it. For then you will make your way prosperous, and then you will have good success.* (Josh 1:8). Wow! Joshua chewed on the words given to him by God through

Moses and thus he found success. Should we not learn this art of meditation of focusing on Biblical principles and bear much fruit?

2. Scripture Passages for Focusing on Biblical Principles
    a) Joshua 1:1-9
    b) Psalm 19:7-14
    c) Psalm 119:1-176
    d) Jeremiah 15:16
    e) John 6:63-69
    f) Acts 17:11
    g) II Timothy 3:14-17
    h) Hebrews 4:12

E. The Saint Paul Model: Becoming like Christ

1. From the Life of Paul the Apostle
    Here we find the example of meditating or becoming like Christ from the life of Paul who said, *"set your mind on things above, not on things on the earth"* (Col. 3:2). Paul taught others to follow his example by thinking on *whatsoever things are true, whatever things are noble, whatever things are just, whatever things are pure, whatever things are lovely, whatever things are of a good report, if there is any virtue and if there is anything praise worthy – meditate on these things* (Phil. 4:8). Perhaps, we like Paul, could become so heavenly minded that we become of earthly good!

2. Scripture Passages on Becoming Like Christ
    a) Galatians 2:19-21
    b) Philippians 2:5-12
    c) Colossians1:14-23
    d) Colossians 3:1-11
    e) I Thessalonians 5:16-24
    f) II Timothy 2:15
    g) Philemon 4:21

F. The Timothy Model: Meditating on Your Calling and Giftings

1. From the Life of Young Timothy the Disciple
    The Timothy Model reminds you to consider God's unique calling in your life and the reason He has gifted you for service. Remember the admonition, *Do not neglect the gift that is in you ...meditate on these things; give yourself entirely to them, that your progress may be evident to all* (I Tim. 4:14,15). We too can grasp a clearer vision of what the Lord has for us if we will pause, reflect and meditate on God's mission for our life and therefore achieve greater effectiveness just as young Timothy was urged to do.

2.   Scripture Passages on Meditating on Your Gifts
      a)   Acts 13:1-4
      b)   Romans 1:11-16
      c)   Romans 11:29 – 12:1-8
      d)   I Corinthians 12:1-11
      e)   Ephesians 4:7-16
      f)   I Timothy 4:11-16
      g)   II Timothy 4:1,2

G.   The Haggai Model: Considering Your Failures

1.   From the Life of Haggai the Prophet
      In learning to meditate as Haggai did, we look at our problems, failures and sins and *"Consider Your Ways"* (Hag. 1:5, 7). Haggai motivates us to look at our shortcomings, change our thinking, and then change our ways. By considering the flaws we can learn not to repeat them.
2.   Scripture Passages About Problem Solving
      a)   Haggai 1:3-11
      b)   Haggai 2:14-19
      c)   Acts 6:1-7
      d)   Acts 15:1-27
      e)   Romans 10:17-21
      f)   I Corinthians 5:1-13
      g)   I John 1:7-2:11

H.   The Asaph Model: Meditating on God's Intervention

1.   From the Life of the Psalmist Asaph
      Asaph wrote 12 psalms that exalt the Lord for His interventions in his life. What God did for Asaph in the past, (and you and I also) will present a key of encouragement for difficult times for the future. *I will remember the works of the Lord; surely I will remember Your wonders of old. I will also meditate on all Your work, and talk of Your deeds* (Ps. 77:11, 12). Through this model you will be encouraged to record significant answers to prayer so you can remember God's faithful ways.
2.   Scripture Passages on God's Intervention
      a)   Psalm 3
      b)   Psalm 50
      c)   Psalm 77
      d)   Psalm 79
      e)   Psalm 82

      f)   Psalms 90

      g)   Acts 9:20-25

I.   The Malachi Model: Meditating on God's Name

1.   From the Life of Malachi, The Last Old Testament Prophet
Here we find a model of meditating on the names of God. *Then those who feared the Lord spoke to one another, and the Lord listened and heard them; so a book of remembrance was written before Him for those who fear the Lord and who meditate on His name* (Mal 3:16). Each name of God depicts a unique character or task of God that teaches us more of who He is and how He relates to us. Practicing the Malachi Model draws us into a greater trust relationship with the one who holds one hand.

2.   Scripture Passages for Meditating on the Names of God
    a)   Exodus 3:14,15
    b)   Exodus 33:18 – 34:8
    c)   Psalm 138:1-8
    d)   Malachi 3:16 – 4:2
    e)   Matthew 6:9-13
    f)   John 4:19-26
    g)   I John 2:12

J.   The Sons of Korah Model: Contemplating Intimacy with God

1.   From the Life the Sons of Korah as Portrayed in the Psalms
The Sons of Korah Model focuses on knowing God intimately. Twelve descriptive psalms are attributed to the sons of Korah who declared, '*We have thought, O God, on Your loving kindness, in the midst of Your temple*' (Ps. 48:9). These Psalmists loved and longed to know god more deeply. This generation was different from their patriarchal Korah, who was judged by God for not coming into the sanctuary of God. But the sons cried out, "*As the deer pants for the water brooks, so pants my soul for you, O God. My soul thirsts for God, for the living God*" (Ps. 12:1, 2). Oh yes, let's follow the next generation and hunger for His presence and meditate on the call to greater intimacy with God.

2.   Scripture Passages on Intimacy with God
    a)   Psalm 2
    b)   Psalm 46:1-11
    c)   Psalm 84
    d)   Matthew 6:1-34
    e)   John 15:1-7
    f)   John 17:1-26
    g)   I John 2:1-18
    h)   I John 4:7-21

III. PRACTICAL GUIDELINES

A. Seven Guidelines for Meditating on God's Word [38]
Teachings of Dr. Sam Storms – Founder of Enjoying God Ministries

1. Prepare
   It helps to begin by rehearsing in one's mind the presence of God. Perhaps reading and reflecting on Psalm 139:1-10 will help. Focus your attention on the inescapable presence, the intimate nearness of God.

   Issues of *posture, time,* and *place* are secondary, but not unimportant. The only rule would be: *do whatever is most conducive to concentration.* If a posture is uncomfortable, change it. If a particular time of day or night is inconvenient, change it. If the place you have chosen exposes you to repeated interruptions and distractions, move it. Now select your text.

2. Peruse
   By this I mean, read, repeat the reading, write it out, re-write it, etc. Peter Toon takes this approach:

   "So I read aloud slowly the verse(s) chosen. One method is to notice the punctuation and to slow down and breathe more slowly for the commas and even more slowly for the periods, so I read aloud softly but clearly so that I may 'taste' the flavor of the word and may also hear the gracious sound of the word. At the same time, my eyes see the content of the word, and I read again – gently dwelling on each word, each phrase, and each sentence"

   We must keep in mind the difference between *informative* reading of the Scriptures and *formative* reading. The former focuses on the gathering of information, the increase of knowledge, the collection and memorization of data. The purpose of the latter is to **be formed** or **shaped** by the text, through the work of the Holy Spirit. With informative reading, I am in control of the text. With formative reading, the text controls me. With formative reading, writes Toon: [39]

"I do not hold the Bible in my hand in order to analyze, dissect or gather information from it. Rather I hold it in order to let my Master penetrate the depths of my being with his Word and thus facilitate inner moral and spiritual transformation. I am there in utter dependence upon our God – who is the Father to whom I pray, the son through whom I pray, and the Holy Spirit in whom I pray." [40]

3. Picture
    Apply your imagination and senses to the truth of the text. Envision yourself personally engaged in the relationship or encounter or experience of which the text speaks. Hear, feel, taste, smell, and see the truths God has revealed.

    The purpose of the imagination is not, as some have argued, to create our own reality. Our imagination is a function of our minds whereby we experience more intimately and powerfully the reality God has created.

4. Ponder
    Reflect on the truth of the Word; brood over the truth of the text; absorb it, soak in it, as you turn it over and over in your mind. By all means, *internalize and personalize the passage.*

5. Pray
    It is difficult to know when meditation moves into prayer. It isn't really that important. But at some point, take the truth as the Holy Spirit has illumined it and pray it back to God, whether in petition, thanksgiving, or intercession or reflection.

6. Praise
    Worship the Lord for who He is and what He has done and how it has been revealed in Scripture. Meditation ought always to lead us into adoration and celebration of God.

7. Practice
    Commit yourself to *doing* what the Word commands. The aim of meditation is moral transformation. The aim of contemplation is obedience. See Josh. 1:8; Ps. 119:11.

B. **In Simple Terms**

    1. Remember
    2. Think on these things
    3. Ponder deeply
    4. Behold the rich love of God

5. Muse on the works of thy hands
6. Meditate
7. Consider
8. Let the mind of Christ be in you
9. Set your mind on things above
10. Let the Word of Christ dwell in you richly

IV. BENEFITS OF MEDITATIVE PRAYER

A. The Benefits of Meditation [41]

1. You gain insight and instruction of truth (Ps. 119:99 – II Tim. 2:7)
2. You get a positive outlook on life (Ps. 104:34)
3. You deepen your love for the Scriptures and God (Ps. 119:97)
4. You become prosperous as you apply the insights gained (Josh. 1:8)
5. You grow and become stable in the Christian life (Ps. 1:2,3; John 15:4)
6. You develop a strong prayer life (John 15:7)
7. You are motivated to ministry (I Sam. 12:24; I Tim. 4:15)
8. You are motivated to repent and live better (Ps. 39:3 – Rev. 2:5)
9. You find the peace of God (Phil. 4:8,9)
10. You get a clear focus to guide you in making decisions (Matt. 6:33 – Col. 3:2)
11. You focus your life on Christ (Heb. 12:3 – I John 3:1)
12. You worship God in His majestic Glory (Deut. 4:39)

B. The Blessings of Meditation

1. Divine Protection: Psalm 91:1
2. Heart's Desire: Psalm 37:4
3. Joy of the Lord: Psalm 104:34
4. Peace of God: Isaiah 26:3
5. Overcoming Anger: Psalm 4:4
6. Overcoming Fear: Deut. 7:17-19
7. Overcoming Sin: Psalm 119:11
8. Renewed Mind: Romans 12:2
9. Stability: Psalm 37:31
10. Wisdom: Psalm 49:3

V. CONCLUDING THOUGHTS

Yet there are many valid diversifications in Biblical meditation. This exists because there is a great diversity of need, background, cultures, gifts and callings. Yes, there are different appropriate aspects of Christian Meditation.

A. Diversities of Models

1. Different motivations
2. Different thought processes
3. Different rules for contemplation
4. Different things to think about
5. Different results needed in our lives

B. More than One Way to Meditate

1. A time to think quietly about God the Creator
2. A time to think practically about God the Problem-solver
3. A time to examine our principles
4. A time to look without at the world in wonder
5. A time to look at the past and remember
6. A time to look to the future and plan
7. A time to face our failures and do better
8. A time to examine our success and go on

C. Summation: The Goal and the Source

Yes there are distinctives just as these different personalities and gifts and callings in the body of Christ. Meditation is an invitation into a dynamic process that has the power to change your thought life and this change the rest of your life. It will help you develop deeper communion with God, encourage your growth in the fruit of the Spirit (character) and be used to unlock God's power source to enable you to serve Him more fully.

Although each model of meditation takes a different face, a different gaze, or even clothing, there are traits and similarities that are common to all of these presented. Simply put, God Himself is the goal and source of our meditation.

Reflection Questions
Lesson Nine: Christian Meditative Prayer

Answers to these questions can be found in the back of the study guide.

1. Read Romans 8:15-16 silently. Now read the passage aloud, personalizing it (For I have received...). [42] Think about these questions:

   a. To what were we once slaves?

   b. Who has adopted us?

   c. How can we know this for sure?

   d. Why are we free from fear?

2. Narrow it down. Choose one of these words to ponder: Slavery, Fear, Adoption, Spirit, Abba. Again write down your significant thoughts. Ask:

   a. What does it mean?

   b. Why should I understand it?

   c. What is God saying about it?

3. Mentally release distracting thoughts as you personalize this aspect of your relationship with God. Ask:

   a. What do you want me to know Lord?

   b. What are you saying?

   c. Who am I and who are you in light of this?

Lesson Ten:
The Fasted Life

I. THE ORIGINS OF FASTING

A. From the Old Testament

1. The Life of Moses
    The first mention of the discipline of fasting in Scripture is the 40-day fast of Moses when God met with him on Mt. Sinai (Ex. 34:28 – Dt. 9:9). There he received directions about building the tabernacle and the Ten Commandments. Moses did a second 40-day fast (Dt. 9:18) during the time the tablets of stone were replaced.

2. Historical Development
    The verb 'fasting' comes from the Hebrew term *tsum*, which refers to self-denial. The noun, *tsum*, means voluntary abstinence from food. Most scholars believe fasting began as a loss of appetite during times of great distress and pressure.
    a) Hannah – I Sam. 1:7
        She was greatly distressed due to her barrenness and *wept and did not eat.*
    b) King Ahab – I Kings. 21:4
        When he failed to purchase Naboth's vineyard he *would eat no food.*
    c) David – II Sam. 3:25
        David used fasting to express his grief at Abner's death.

3. Day of Atonement – The Required Fast
    The only required yearly fast was on the Day of Atonement when the High Priest would offer acts of sacrifice for the sins of the people. (Lev.16:11, 15, 21, 29) Lev. 16:29 states *"and this shall be a permanent statute for you: in the tenth day of the month, you shall humble your souls, and not do any work".* The people fasted for self-examination and to demonstrate remorse.

4. Expression of Grief and Desperation
    Fasting became a natural expression of human grief and a custom to fend off the anger of God. Eventually, fasting became a way for making ones petition effective to God.

    When fasting became a national call it was used to seek divine favor, protection or to circumvent the historical judgment of God. Therefore, it became a normal practice for a group of people to combine confession of sin, sorrow, and intercession with fasting.

B.   From the New Testament

1.   By the Pharisees
It is believed that the Pharisees fasted Tuesdays and Thursdays of each week. The Pharisee stood and prayed thus with himself, *"God, I thank you that I am not like other men – extortioners, unjust, adulterers, or even as this tax collector. I fast twice a week. I give tithes of all that I possess"*. (Lk. 18:11,12).

2.   By Disciples of John the Baptist
John the Baptist was a Nazarite from birth (Num. 6:2-8.– Luke. 1:15-17) who came in the spirit of Elijah. A Nazarite was "a person of the vow". Fasting was a part of his lifestyle. Therefore, His disciples followed in His example of sacrificial living (Matt. 9:14-15).

3.   By Jesus Christ
Jesus began His public ministry with an extended fast. He also observed the Jewish yearly fast on the Day of Atonement as part of His heritage. But Jesus gave little specific recorded guidelines to His disciplines concerning fasting. He taught that their fasting should be different from that of the Pharisees in order to be seen by God and not to impress men (Matt. 6:16-18).

4.   The Early Church
The early church practiced fasting, especially when ordaining elders or setting people apart to a special task or ministry (Acts 13:2). Paul and other Christian leaders also practiced fasting regularly (I Cor. 7:5 – II Cor. 6:5).

C.   Accounts from Church History

1.   Epiphanius – Bishop of Salamis born in 315 A.D.
Early in church history, Christians began fasting twice a week, choosing Wednesdays and Fridays to prevent being confused with Pharisees, who fasted Tuesdays and Thursdays. Epiphanius stated, 'who does not know that the fast of the fourth and sixth days of the week are observed by Christians throughout the world?'

2.   In Preparation of Special 'Holy Days'
The practice of fasting for several days before Easter to prepare spiritually for the celebration of Jesus' resurrection was also practiced. Later, this was turned into a time of special seeking of God's face during the time of Lent – A 40 day period prior to Easter. Partial fasting was typically observed. Fasting was also encouraged in the second and third centuries of the church as preparation for water baptism.

3. Fasting in Revival Movements
    The discipline of fasting has long been associated with reforms and revivalistic movements throughout church history. The founders of the monastic movements practiced fasting as a regular part of their lifestyle. Each of the 16th century reformers (and those earlier) also practiced fasting, as did the leaders of the evangelical great awakenings. John Wesley would not ordain a man to ministry unless he fasted two days every week. Jonathan Edwards was known to have fasted before God before he released his now famous message *Sinners in Hands of an Angry God.*

    During the laymen's Prayer Revival in North America in 1859, Christians fasted during their lunch hours and attended prayer meetings. This prayer revival broke out in the large industrial cities of the northeast part of the United States and spread across North America.

    If Charles Finney, noted revivalist, felt the spirit's anointing lift off his life and preaching, he would retreat and fast till it (He) returned!

II. NINE BIBLICAL FASTS [43]

The following material is inspired from the writings of Elmer L. Towns in his book *Fasting for Spiritual Breakthrough.*

A. The Disciples Fast

1. Purpose: *To loose the bands of wickedness* (Is. 58:6) - freeing ourselves and others from addictions to sin.
2. Key Verse: Mt. 17:21 – *This kind goeth not out but by prayer and fasting.* KJV
3. Background: Jesus cast out a demon from a boy whom the disciples had failed to help. Apparently they had not taken seriously enough the way Satan had his claws set in the youth. The implication is that Jesus' disciples could have performed this exorcism had they been willing to undergo the discipline of fasting. Modern disciples also often make light of 'besetting sins' that could be cast out if we were serious enough to take part in such a self-denying practice as fasting - hence the term "Disciple's Fast."

B. The Ezra Fast

1. Purpose: To *undo the heavy burdens* (Is. 58:6) – to solve problems, inviting the Holy Spirit's aid in lifting loads and overcoming barriers that keep ourselves and our loved ones from walking joyfully with the Lord.

2. Key Verse: Ezra 8:23 – *So we fasted and entreated our God for this, and He answered our prayer.*

3. Background: Ezra the priest was charged with restoring the Law of Moses among the Jews as they rebuilt the city of Jerusalem by permission of Artaxerxes, King of Persia, where God's people had been held captive. Despite this permission, Israel's enemies opposed them. Burdened with embarrassment about having to ask the Persian King for an army to protect them, Ezra fasted and prayed for an answer.

C. The Samuel Fast

1. Purpose: *To let the oppressed* (physically and spiritually) *go free* (Is. 58:6) – for revival and soul winning, to identify with people everywhere enslaved literally or by sin and to pray to be used of God to bring people out of the kingdom of darkness and into God's marvelous light.

2. Key Verse: I Sam. 7:6 – *So they gathered together at Mizpah, drew water, and poured it out before the Lord, and they fasted that day, and said there, "We have sinned against the Lord".*

3. Background: Samuel led God's people in a fast to celebrate the return of the Ark of the Covenant from its captivity by the Philistines, and to pray that Israel might be delivered from the sin that allowed the Ark to be captured in the first place.

D. The Elijah Fast

1. Purpose: *To break every yoke* (Is. 58:6) - conquering the mental and emotional problems that would control our lives, and returning the control to the Lord.

2. Key Verse: I Kings 19:4, 8 – *He himself went a day's journey into the wilderness...He arose and ate and drank; and he went in the strength of that food forty days and forty nights.*

3. Background: Although Scripture does not call this a formal "fast," Elijah deliberately went without food when he fled from Queen Jezebel's threat to kill him. After this self-imposed deprivation, God sent an angel to minister to Elijah in the wilderness.

E.   The Widow's Fast

1.   Purpose: *To share (our) bread with the hungry* and to care for the poor (Is. 58:7) – to meet the humanitarian needs of others.
2.   Key Verse: I Kings 17:16 - *The jar of flour was not used up and the jug of oil did not run dry, in keeping with the word of the Lord spoken by Elijah.* NIV
3.   Background: God sent the prophet Elijah to a poor starving widow – ironically, so the widow could provide food for Elijah. Just as Elijah's presence resulted in food for the widow of Zarephath, so presenting ourselves before God in prayer and fasting can relieve hunger today.

F.   The Saint Paul Fast

1.   Purpose: To allow God's *light (to) break forth like the morning* (Is. 58:8), bringing clearer perspective and insight as we make crucial decisions.
2.   Key Verse: Acts 9:9 – *And he (Saul, or Paul) was three days without sight, and neither ate nor drank.*
3.   Background: Saul of Tarsus, who became known as Paul after his conversion to Christ, was struck blind by the Lord in his act of persecuting Christians. He not only was without literal sight, but he also had no clue about what direction his life was to take. After going without food and praying for three days, Paul was visited by the Christian Ananias, and both his eyesight and his vision of the future were restored.

G.   The Daniel Fast

1.   Purpose: So *thine health shall spring forth* (Is. 58:8, KJV) – to gain a healthier life or for healing.
2.   Key Verse: Dan. 1:8 – *Daniel purposed in his heart that he would not defile himself with the King's choice food or wine which he drank.*
3.   Background: Daniel and his three fellow Hebrew captives demonstrated in Babylonian captivity that keeping themselves from pagan foods God had guided them not to eat, made them more healthy than others in the king's court.

H.   The John the Baptist Fast

1.   Purpose: That *your righteousness shall go before you* (Is. 58:8) – that our testimonies and influence for Jesus will be enhanced before others.

2. Key Verse: Luke 1:15 – *He shall be great in the sight of the Lord, and shall drink neither wine nor strong drink.* KJV

3. Background: Because John the Baptist was the forerunner of Jesus, he took the 'Nazarite' vow that required him to 'fast' from or avoid wine and strong drink. This was part of John's purposefully adopted lifestyle that designated him as one set apart for a special mission.

I.   The Esther Fast

1. Purpose: That the glory of the Lord will protect us from the evil one (Is. 58:8).

2. Key Verses: Es. 4:16, 5:2 – *Fast for me...(and) my maids and I will fast...(and) I will go to the king...(and) she found favor in his sight.*

3. Background: Queen Esther, a Jewess in a pagan court, risked her life to save her people from threatened destruction by Ahasuerus (Xerxes), king of Persia. Prior to appearing before the king to petition him to save the Jews, Esther, her attendants, and her cousin Mordecai all fasted to appeal to God for His protection.

III.   FASTING ACCOMPANIED BY... [44]

A.   Biblical References

1. Prayer
   a) Ezra 8:23 – *So we fasted and entreated our God for this, and He answered our prayer.*
   b) Neh. 1:4 – *So it was, when I heard these words, that I sat down and wept, and mourned for many days; I was fasting and praying before the God of heaven.*
   c) Ps. 35:13 – *But as for me, when they were sick, my clothing was sackcloth; I humbled myself with fasting; and my prayer would return to my own heart.*
   d) Dan. 9:3 – *Then I set my face toward the Lord God to make request by prayer and supplications, with fasting, sackcloth, and ashes.*
   e) Luke 5:33 – *Then they said to Him, 'Why do the disciples of John fast often and make prayers, and likewise those of the Pharisees, but Yours eat and drink'?*

2. Worship
   a) Neh. 9:1-3 – *Now on the twenty-fourth day of this month the children of Israel were assembled with fasting, in sackcloth, and with dust on their heads. Then those of Israelite lineage separated themselves from all foreigners; and they stood and confessed their sins and the iniquities of their fathers. And*

they stood up in their place and read from the Book of the Law of the Lord their God for one-fourth of the day; and for another fourth they confessed and worshipped the Lord their God.

3. Confession of Sin

   a) I Sam. 7:6 – *So they gathered together at Mizpah, drew water, and poured it out before the Lord. And they fasted that day, and said there, "We have sinned against the Lord." And Samuel judged the children of Israel at Mizpah.*

   b) Neh. 9:1-3 – *Now on the twenty-fourth day of this month the children of Israel were assembled with fasting, in sackcloth, and with dust on their heads. Then those of Israelite lineage separated themselves from all foreigners; and they stood and confessed their sins and the iniquities of their fathers. And they stood up in their place and read from the Book of the Law of the Lord their God for one-fourth of the day; and for another fourth they confessed and worshipped the Lord their God.*

4. Humiliation

   a) Dt. 9:18 – *And I fell down before the Lord, as at the first, forty days and forty nights; I neither ate bread nor drank water, because of all your sin which you committed in doing wickedly in the sight of the Lord, to provoke Him to anger.*

   b) Ps. 35:13 – *But as for me, when they were sick, my clothing was sack-cloth; I humbled myself with fasting; and my prayer would return to my own heart.*

   c) Ps. 69:10 – *When I wept and chastened my soul with fasting, that became my reproach.*

   d) I Kings 21:27 – *So it was, when Ahab heard those words, that he tore his clothes and put sackcloth on his body, and fasted and lay in sackcloth, and went about mourning.*

   e) Neh. 9:1 – *Now on the twenty-fourth day of this month the children of Israel were assembled with fasting, in sackcloth, and with dust on their heads.*

5. Reading the Scriptures

   a) Neh. 9:1-3 – *Now on the twenty-fourth day of this month the children of Israel were assembled with fasting, in sackcloth, and with dust on their heads. Then those of Israelite lineage separated themselves from all foreigners; and they stood and confessed their sins and the iniquities of their fathers. And they stood up in their place and read from the Book of the Law of the Lord their God for one-fourth of the day; and for another fourth they confessed and worshipped the Lord their God.*

   b) Jer. 36:6 – *You go, therefore, and read from the scroll which you have written at my instruction, the words of the Lord, in*

99

the hearing of the people in the Lord's house on the day of fasting. And you shall also read them in the hearing of all Judah who come from their cities.

    c)   Jer. 36:10 – *Then Baruch read from the book the words of Jeremiah in the house of the Lord, in the chamber of Gemariah the son of Shaphan the scribe, in the upper court at the entry of the New Gate of the Lord's house, in the hearing of all the people.*

6.   Mourning

    a)   II Sam. 1:12 – *And they mourned and wept and fasted until evening for Saul and for Jonathan his son, for the people of the Lord and for the house of Israel, because they had fallen by the sword.*

    b)   I Kings 21:27 – *So it was, when Ahab heard those words, that he tore his clothes and put sackcloth on his body, and fasted and lay in sackcloth, and went about mourning.*

    c)   Esther 4:3 – *And in every province where the king's command and decree arrived, there was great mourning among the Jews, with fasting, weeping, and wailing; and many lay in sackcloth and ashes.*

    d)   Neh. 1:4 – *So it was, when I heard these words, that I sat down and wept, and mourned for many days; I was fasting and praying before the God of heaven*

    e)   Joel 2:12 – *"Now, therefore", says the Lord, "Turn to Me with all your heart, with fasting, with weeping, and with mourning".*

    f)   Ezra 10:6 – *Then Ezra rose up from before the house of God, and went into the chamber of Jehohanan the son of Eliashib; and when he came there, he ate no bread and drank no water, for he mourned because of the guilt of those from the captivity.*

7.   Weeping

    a)   II Sam. 1:12 – *And they mourned and wept and fasted until evening for Saul and for Jonathan his son, for the people of the Lord and for the house of Israel, because they had fallen by the sword.*

    b)   Neh. 1:4 – *So it was, when I heard these words, that I sat down and wept, and mourned for many days; I was fasting and praying before the God of heaven.*

    c)   Esther 4:3 – *And in every province where the king's command and decree arrived, there was great mourning among the Jews, with fasting, weeping, and wailing; and many lay in sackcloth and ashes.*

    d)   Ps. 69:10 – *When I wept and chastened my soul with fasting, that became my reproach.*

    e)   Joel 2:12 – *"Now, therefore", says the Lord, "Turn to me with all your heart, with fasting, with weeping, and with mourning."*

8.   Abstinence from Sexual Relationships

a)   I Cor. 7:5 – *Do not deprive one another except with consent for a time, that you may give yourselves to fasting and prayer; and come together again so that Satan does not tempt you because of your lack of self-control.*

B.   Contemporary Issues to Consider

In the 21st Century, there are several additional issues that could be considered as a form of sacrifice, abstinence, or 'fasting' before God. The following are not abstaining from food for spiritual purposes. But they are contemporary issues of today's society that could be considered as a form of fasting for a period of time to seek God's face.

1.   Entertainment –
Movies, videos, television, radio, video games, secular dancing, etc.
2.   Athletic Events –
Professional sports, athletic events, other forms of recreation, etc.
3.   Reading Material –
Magazines, books, newspapers, other news media, even Christian fiction.
4.   Computers –
Internet activity, E-mail, Games, etc.
5.   Speech –
Phone calls, amount of talking, limiting topics of conversation, a special vow of silence, etc.
6.   Dress –
Avoiding certain types and styles of clothing, or the wearing of specific types and styles of clothing, etc.
7.   Foods and Drinks –
Partial fasting - limiting intake of specific foods or drinks.
8.   Sleep –
Early morning prayer, all night prayer vigils, prayer watches at various hours, etc.
9.   Social Functions –
Limiting outside engagements, conferences, seminars and even normal church activities for short specific periods, times of purposeful isolation.
10.   Work Schedule –
Taking hours or days off from secular work or even ministry engagements to seek God's face, etc.

IV.   THE BRIDEGROOM FAST

A.   In the Last Days

1.   Joel 2:28,29 – *And it will come about after this that I will pour out My Spirit on all mankind; And your sons and daughters will prophesy, Your old men will dream dreams, your young men will see visions. And even on the male and female servants I will pour out My Spirit in those days.*

2.   Desolation – Consecration - Restoration
The book of Joel paints us a picture of the last days period in which seeking God's face with fasting (Joel 2:12) precedes the great latter rain outpouring (Joel 2:25) and a worldwide display of His Glory (Joel 2:30-32).

B.   The Return of Christ

1.   Acts 1:1 – *This account I composed, Theophilus, about all that Jesus began to do and teach.*

2.   Second Coming
Neither, though, the outpouring of the Spirit nor even the great restoration or reformation of the church is our primary goal. It is nothing less than the reappearance of our Glorious Lord, Jesus Christ.

C.   A Lovesick Heart

Matthew 9:15 – *And Jesus said to them, "The attendants of the bridegroom cannot mourn as long as the bride groom is with them can they? But the days will come when the bridegroom is taken away from them and they will fast."*

As Mike Bickle says [45] – Jesus was saying that fasting is directly related to experiencing the presence of the Bridegroom. And that is, in essence, His highest purpose for this discipline: to develop in us a greater spiritual capacity for intimacy with our Bridegroom God.

Jesus assured those questioning Him that when He was taken away (through His death on the cross) they would fast because of their grief. He knew that His disciples had grown so accustomed to enjoying His presence that after He was gone they would mourn the loss of it and begin to yearn for a sense of closeness to Him. Yearning for the one you love is commonly called lovesickness. Can you imagine whole-hearted lovers of Jesus today becoming so filled with holy lovesickness that they freely choose to live fasted lifestyles? This is what Jesus was prophetically speaking of.

You may be wondering what practical results you can expect from the Bridegroom fast. Here are three of them:

1. You will receive more revelation of God while pouring over His Word. Imagine receiving more revelation of the beauty of God that fascinates our hearts!
2. You will receive a greater measure of revelation in an accelerated way. When people tell me, "I just can't wait to receive more from God," I tell them to add fasting to their loving meditation on the Word. This type of fasting speeds up the process of receiving from God. It also speeds up the process of getting rid of old mind-sets, old strongholds and hard-heartedness.
3. The revelation we receive will touch us at a deeper level. A heart tenderized in love is the greatest gift the Holy Spirit can work in a worshipper. To live feeling loved by God and feeling a reciprocal, passionate love for Him is the most exhilarating form of existence. If you want to experience more of Jesus in a deeper way, start fasting with a focus on Jesus as the Bridegroom. The Holy Spirit gives grace and revelation to His people who aren't afraid to cry out for it. And when you respond to His wooing and embrace a Bridegroom fast – God's feast for His bride - you will mature and enter into intimacy with the Bridegroom. Then you will be able to assume your true identity as the bride of Christ and be fully prepared for His return.

D. A New Order and Motivation

1. A New Day
    A new day has dawned. The old rites and legal bondage of performing to earn entrance and acceptance before God no longer remain. We enter freely through the blood of Jesus Christ. Though Jesus disciples would fast again, they would never fast as they had before. They would fast out of a new heart and a new motivation.
2. From Arthur Wallis – *God's Chosen Fast* [46]
    "Before the Bridegroom left them, He promised that He would come again to receive them to Himself. The church still awaits the midnight cry, 'Behold, the bridegroom! Come out to meet him' (Matt. 25:6). It is this age of the church that is the period of the absent Bridegroom. It is this age of the church to which our Master referred when He said 'then they will fast.' The time is now!

"These words of Jesus were prophetic. The first Christians fulfilled them, and so have many saintly men and women of succeeding generations. Where are those who fulfill them today? Alas, they are few and far between, the exception rather than the rule, to the great loss of the church.

"A new generation, however, is arising. There is concern in the hearts of many for the recovery of apostolic power. But how can we recover apostolic power while neglecting apostolic practice? How can we expect the power to flow if we do not prepare the channels? Fasting is a God appointed means for the flowing of His grace and power that we can't afford to neglect any longer.

"The fast of this age is not merely an act of mourning for Christ's absence, but an act of preparation for His return. May those prophetic words, 'Then will they fast', be finally fulfilled in this generation. It will be a fasting and praying church that will hear the thrilling cry, 'Behold, the Bridegroom!' Tears shall then be wiped away, and the fast be followed by the feast at the marriage supper of the Lamb."

The Spirit and the Bride say, "Come". Surely I am coming soon. Amen, Come, Lord Jesus! (Rev. 22:17, 20)

3. The Contemplative
    The contemplative fasts out of a lovesick heart! Passion for His presence, longing for His return, brokenness as over a lover who has left, waiting for His return is now the new motivation of the Bridegroom fast!

Reflection Questions
Lesson Ten: The Fasted Life

Answers to these questions can be found in the back of the study guide.

If the Lord is speaking to you about a prolonged fast, set time aside to wait on Him in fasting and prayer. Ask the Lord for the particular theme or issue you need the Lord to intervene in. (Perhaps a deepening of sanctified life; praying for a particular friend, church or nation; seeking the Lord over direction; etc.)

1. Over the course of your fast, journal your thoughts, feelings, revelations, impressions, and scriptures the Lord prompted you with.

2. In the leaders guide, *Experiencing God* by Claude King, [47] he lists 10 questions to help recognize God's work in your lives. In your journal keep these questions close to your heart as you fast and pray.

    a. What has God revealed to you about Himself?

    b. What has God revealed to you about His purposes?

    c. What has God revealed to you about His ways?

    d. What has God done in your life or through your life that has caused you to experience His presence?

    e. What scripture has God used to speak to you about Himself, His purposes or His ways?

f. What particular person or concern has God given you a burden to pray for? What has He guided you to pray for in this situation?

g. What has God done through circumstances that have given you a sense of His timing or direction concerning any aspect of His will?

h. What word of guidance or truth do you sense God has spoken to you through another believer?

i. What adjustment is God leading you to make in your life?

j. What acts of obedience have you accomplished this week? What further steps of obedience do you know God wants you to take?

Lesson Eleven:
Towards A Greater Union

I. THE ALPHA AND THE OMEGA

A. Our Beginning – Our Ending
The following are scripture verses on Christ being our beginning and ending of all things.

1. Rev. 1:8 – *"I am the Alpha and the Omega", says the Lord God, "Who is and Who was and Who is to come, the Almighty".*
2. Isa. 41:4 – *Who has performed and accomplished it, calling forth the generations from the beginning? I, the Lord, am the first, and with the last. I am He.*
3. Rev. 21:6 – *And He said to me, "It is done. I am the Alpha and the Omega, the beginning and the end. I will give to the one who thirsts from the spring of the water of life without cost."*
4. Rev. 22:13 – *I am the Alpha and the Omega, the first and the last, the beginning and the end.*

B. In Him Is Life
Read the following foundational verses that declare that our life is in Christ Jesus.

1. John 1:4 – *In Him was life; and the life was the light of men.*
2. I John 5:12-13 – *He who has the Son has the life; he who does not have the Son of God does not have the life. These things I have written to you who believe in the name of the Son of God, in order that you may know that you have eternal life.*
3. Lev. 17:11 – *For the life of the flesh is in the blood, and I have given it to you on the altar to make atonement for your souls; for it is the blood by reason of the life that makes atonement.*

C. *Abide In Christ* – By Andrew Murray [48]

He that abideth in me, and I in him, the same bringeth forth much fruit. Herein is my Father glorified, that ye bear much fruit. Jn. 15:5,8.

"We all know what fruit is – The produce of the branch, by which men are refreshed and nourished. The fruit is not for the branch, but for those who come to carry it away. As soon as the fruit is ripe, the branch gives it off, to commence afresh its work of beneficence, and anew prepare its fruit for another season. A fruit-bearing tree lives not for itself, but wholly for those to whom its fruit brings refreshment and life. And so the branch exists only and entirely for the sake of the fruit. To make glad the heart of the husbandman is its object, its safety, and its glory.

"Beautiful is the image of the believer, abiding in Christ! He not only grows in strength, the union with the Vine becoming ever surer and firmer, he also bears fruit, yea, much fruit. He has the power to offer that to others of which they can eat and live. Amid all who surround Him, he becomes like a tree of life, of which they can taste and be refreshed. He is in his circle a center of life and of blessing, and that simply because he abides in Christ, and receives from Him the Spirit and the life of which he can impart to others. Learn thus, if you would bless others, to abide in Christ, and that if you do abide, you shall surely bless. As surely as the branch abiding in a fruitful vine bears fruit, so surely, yea, *much more surely*, will a soul abiding in Christ with His fullness of blessing be made a blessing."

D. *The Seeking Heart* – Francois de Fenelon [49]

"Your spiritual walk is a little too restless and uneasy. Simply trust God. If you come to Him, He will give you all that you need to serve Him. You really need to believe that God keeps His word. The more you trust Him, the more He will be able to give you. If you were lost in an uncrossable desert, bread would fall from heaven for you alone.

"Fear nothing but to fail God. And do not even fear that so much that you let is upset you. Learn to live with your failures, and bear with the failures of your neighbors. Do you know what would be best for you? Stop trying to appear so mentally and spiritually perfect to God and man. There is a lot of refined selfishness and complacency in not allowing your faults to be revealed. Be simple with God. He loves to communicate Himself to simple people. Live day by day, not in your own strength, but by completely surrendering to God."

II. THE SECRET OF THE HIDDEN TREASURES

A. The Field of God

1. Matt. 13:44 – *The kingdom of heaven is like a treasure hidden in the field, which a man found and hid; and from joy over it he goes and sells all that he has, and buys that field.*
2. I Cor. 3:9 – *For we are God's fellow workers; you are God's field, God's building.*

B. Christ in Us

1. Col. 1:27 – *To whom God willed to make known what is the riches of the glory of this mystery among the Gentiles, which is Christ in you, the hope of glory.*
2. I Cor 3:16 – *Do you not know that you are a temple of God, and that the Spirit of God dwells in you?*

C. *Hidden Treasure – A Center of Quiet* by David Runcorn [50]
"Jesus always taught that the most important things in life are not found on the surface. Although clues are everywhere, the Kingdom of God is never so revealed as to be obvious. It is like treasure hidden in a field or the pearl hidden, improbably, in the rough hard shell of an oyster. Its power is concealed in the tiniest things – the seed that will one day be the greatest of trees, the small piece of leaven that will swell the whole batch of dough. And the Kingdom of God is revealed to those who are explorers, who knock, and seek and ask and dig beneath the surface until the treasure of life is uncovered. Even the secrets of our lives, says Paul, are 'hidden' with Christ in God. (Col. 3:3)"

D. Go Searching

1. Isa. 55:6 – *Seek the Lord while He may be found; Call upon Him while He is near.*
2. Isa. 64:7 – *And there is no one who calls on Thy name, Who arouses himself to take hold of Thee; For Thou hast hidden Thy face from us, and hast delivered us into the power of our iniquities.*
3. Col. 3:3 – *For you have died and your life is hidden with Christ in God.*
4. Rom. 14:17 – *For the kingdom of God is not eating and drinking, but righteousness and peace and joy in the Holy Spirit.*

III. PRACTICE THE PRESENCE
The following are principles concerning the presence of God taken from the life of Brother Lawrence.

A. The Means of Acquiring
Brother Lawrence – *The Practice of the Presence of God* [51]

"The first means is a new life, received by salvation through the blood of Christ.

"The second is faithfully practicing God's presence. This must always be done gently, humbly, and lovingly, without giving way to anxiety or problems.

"The soul's eyes must be kept on God, particularly when something is being done in the outside world. Since much time and effort are needed to perfect this practice, one should not be discouraged by failure. Although the habit is difficult to form, it is a source of divine pleasure once it is learned.

"It is proper that the heart – which is the first to live and which dominates all the other parts of the body – should be the first and the last to love God. The heart is the beginning and the end of all our spiritual and bodily actions and, generally speaking, of everything we do in our lives. It is, therefore, the heart whose attention must carefully focus on God.

"In the beginning of this practice, it would not be wrong to offer short phrases that are inspired by love, such as 'Lord, I am all Yours,' 'God of love, I love You with all my heart', or 'Lord, use me according to Your will'. But remember to keep the mind from wandering or returning to the world. Hold your attention on God alone by exercising your will to remain in God's presence.

"Although this exercise may be difficult at first to maintain, it has marvelous effects on the soul when it is faithfully practiced. It draws the graces of the Lord down in abundance and shows the soul how to see God's presence everywhere with a pure and loving vision, which is the holiest, firmest, easiest, and the most effective attitude for prayer."

B. The Blessings
Brother Lawrence – More from *The Practice of the Presence of God.* [52]

"The first blessing that the soul receives from the practice of the presence of God is that its faith is livelier and more active everywhere in our lives. This is particularly true in difficult times, since it obtains the grace we need to deal with temptation and to conduct ourselves in the world. The soul – accustomed by this exercise to the practice of faith – can actually see and feel God by simply entering His presence.

"It invokes Him easily and obtains what it needs. In so doing, the soul could be said to approach the Blessed, in that it can almost say, "I no longer believe, but I see and experience." Its faith becomes more and more penetrating as it advances through practice.

"The practice of the presence of God strengthens us in hope. Our hope increases as our faith penetrates God's secrets through practice of our holy exercise. The soul discovers in God a beauty infinitely surpassing not only that of bodies that we see on earth, but even that of the angels. Our hope increases and grows stronger, and the amount of good that it expects to enjoy, and that in some degree it tastes, reassures and sustains it.

"This practice causes the will to rejoice at being set apart from the world, setting it aglow with the fire of holy love. This is because the soul is always with God, Who is a consuming fire, Who reduces into powder whatever is opposed to Him. The soul thus inflamed can no longer live except in the presence of its God. This presence produces a holy ardor, a sacred urgency, and a violent desire in the heart to see this God, Who is loved.

"By practicing God's presence and continuously looking at Him, the soul familiarizes itself with Him to the extent that it passes almost its whole life in continual acts of love, praise, confidence, thanksgiving, offering, and petition. Sometimes all this may merge into one single act that does not end, because the soul is always in the ceaseless exercise of God's Divine presence."

IV. CHRIST ALTOGETHER LOVELY

A. Christ Is to Be Loved

From the writings of John Flavel – in the book by Don Milan – *The Lost Passions of Jesus* [53]

John Flavel was born in Worcestershire, England, and was a contemporary of Madame Guyon. His text, Christ Altogether Lovely, was never published, but it was a true example of that passion.

Yes, *He is altogether lovely* – Song of Songs 5:16. The words set forth the transcendent loveliness of the Lord Jesus Christ and naturally resolve themselves into three parts:

1.   Who He is.
2.   What He is.
3.   What He is like.

First, Who He Is:

The Lord Jesus Christ, after whom she had been seeking, for whom she was overcome by love; concerning whom these daughters of

Jerusalem had enquired: whom she had struggled to describe in his particular excellencies. He is the great and excellent subject of whom she here speaks.

Second, What He Is, or What She Claims of Him:

That He is a lovely one. The Hebrew word, which is often translated 'desires,' means 'to earnestly desire, covet, or long after that which is most pleasant, graceful, delectable and admirable.' The original word is both in the abstract, and plural in number, which says that Christ is the very essence of all delights and pleasures, the very soul and substance of them. As all the rivers are gathered into the ocean, which is the meeting-place of all the waters in the world, so Christ is that ocean in which all true delights and pleasures meet.

Third, What He Is Like:

He is altogether lovely, the very part to be desired. He is lovely when taken together, and in every part; as if she had said, 'Look on Him in what respect or particular you wish; cast your eye upon this lovely object, and view Him any way, turn Him in your serious thoughts which way you wish; consider His person, His offices, His works, or any other thing belonging to Him; you will find Him altogether lovely. There is nothing disagreeable in Him, there is nothing lovely without Him.' Hence note, DOCTRINE: That Jesus Christ is the loveliest person souls can set their eyes upon:

Psalm 14:2 – *Thou art fairer than the children of men.*

B. How Christ Is Altogether Lovely

1. He Is Lovely in His Person
   First, He is altogether lovely in His person: He is Deity dwelling in the flesh (John 1:14). The wonderful, perfect union of the divine and human nature in Christ renders Him an object of admiration and adoration to both angels and men (1 Tim. 3:16).
2. He Is Lovely in His Offices
   Secondly, He is altogether lovely in His offices: let us consider for a moment the suitability, fullness, and comforting nature of them.
3. He Is Lovely in His Relations
   Third, He is a lovely Redeemer (Is. 61:1). He came to open the prison-doors to them that are bound. Needs must this Redeemer be a lovely one, if we consider the depth of misery from which He redeemed us, even "from the wrath to come," (I Thess. 1:10).
   a) He is a lovely bridegroom to all that He betroths to himself. How does the church glory in Him, in the words following

my text; *this is my Beloved, and this is my Friend, O ye daughters of Jerusalem.* Heaven and earth cannot show anyone like Him.

b) Christ is altogether lovely, in the relation of an Advocate. I John 2:1 – *If any man sin, we have an advocate with the Father, Jesus Christ the righteous, and he is the Propitiation.* It is He that pleads the cause of believers in heaven. He appears for them in the presence of God, to prevent any new alienation, and to continue the state of friendship and peace between God and us. In this relation Christ is altogether lovely.

c) Christ is altogether lovely in the relation of a friend, for in this relation He is pleased to acknowledge His people (Luke 12:4, 5). There are certain things in which one friend manifests His affection and friendship to another, but there is not one like Christ.

V. UNION WITH CHRIST

A. Visionary Experience – Seven Doorways
Let me recap by telling you again of a revelatory encounter where I saw seven consecutive doorways with words written at the top of each entrance. The following was the list of names I saw.

1. Invitation to the Inward Journey
2. Forgiveness
3. Cleansed by the blood
4. Lowliness of Heart
5. Grace (from God)
6. Mercy (towards men)
7. Union With Christ

B. The Goal of All Things
What Is the Goal of Contemplative Prayer? Richard J. Foster – *Prayer: Finding the Heart's True Home* [54]

To this question the old writers answer with one voice: Union with God.

Juliana of Norwich declares, "The whole reason why we pray is to be united into the vision and contemplation of Him to whom we pray."

Bonaventure, a follower of Saint Francis, says that our final goal is "union with God"; which is a pure relationship where we see "nothing."

113

And Madame Guyon writes, "We come now to the ultimate stage of Christian experience: Divine Union. This cannot be brought about merely by your own experience. Meditation will not bring divine union; neither will love, nor worship, nor your devotion, nor your sacrifice...Eventually is will take an *act of God* to make union a reality."

C. Union with God

1. Union with God does not mean the loss of our individuality. Far from causing any loss of identity, union brings about full personhood. We become all that God created us to be. Contemplatives sometimes speak of their union with God by the analogy of a log in a fire; the glowing log is so united with the fire that it is fire, while, at the same time, it remains wood. Others use the comparison of a white-hot iron in a furnace: "Our personalities are transformed, not lost, in the furnace of God's love."

VI. THE OVERFLOW OF A CONTEMPLATIVE LIFE

The following closing to this teaching comes from the writings of Pat Gastineau's booklet on Contemplative Prayer. [55]

"Ps. 45:1 – *My heart is overflowing with a good theme; I recite my composition concerning the King; My tongue is the pen of a ready writer.* The Living Bible says: 'My heart is overflowing with a beautiful thought: I will write a lovely poem to the King, for I am full of words as the speediest writer pouring out his story.'

"Let us ask the Holy Ghost to fire up longings for Him that would readily find expression. Just as the pen is guided by the human hand, let my tongue be guided by my heart, let it be a pen in the hand of God to glorify the King.

"Oh, Living Joy that has captured my heart! My heart has burst its banks, spilling out as a river flowing from deep within my being."

Reflection Questions
Lesson Eleven: Towards A Greater Union

Answers to these questions can be found in the back of the study guide.

These questions have been taken from the book: *The Soul at Rest.* [56]

1. Protect Your Mind:
   Read the following affirmations based on Ephesians 6:11-18.

   I am protected by the full armor of God.
   I am protected by God's truth.
   I am protected by the righteousness of Jesus Christ Himself.
   I am protected by the gospel of God's peace.
   I am protected by my faith in God from all lies of the evil one.
   I am redeemed by the blood of Jesus Christ.
   I hold in my hands the Word of God to pierce the darkness and radiate God's light.
   The living Christ alone has access to my mind and heart this day.

2. Purify Your Heart:
   Take some time to isolate the motives and intentions of your heart. Let go of any desire other than to see God as He is. Invite God to walk through the rooms of your heart. Allow His gentle Spirit purify and enlighten you as you go.

3. Praise Your Redeemer:
   Read Isaiah 61:1-3 quietly. Write the verses in your prayer journal as if God had just spoken these truths to you personally. Read what you have written aloud, thanking God for each specific thing He holds out. Reflect on each part of the promise. Worship quietly with words of adoration for all God is, based on these verses.

4. Present Yourself to God:
   Be very still and quiet. Gently turn inward to the indwelling Christ. Silently yield yourself to Him. Be Still. Allow the hush of His presence to permeate your mind and heart. Repeat the following verse a few times: *Whom have I in heaven but Thee? And besides Thee, I desire nothing on earth* (Ps. 73:25).

Lesson Twelve:
Walking through the Tabernacle

The following closing lesson becomes a synopsis of much of what we have looked at in previous lessons directing us towards the goal that contemplative prayer is: To personally feed and empower us for effective impact and ministry.

I. GLIMPSES OF DIFFERENT FORMS OF PRAYER

A. Three Models of Prayer

1. Contemplative Prayer
2. Reminding God of His Word
3. Prophetic Intercession

When we wed the contemplative facet of communal prayer with the reminding God of His Word model they couple to form that which can be called Prophetic intercession.

This is a lost art to most of the evangelical and charismatic church. Quieting our souls before God and coming into a place of deep communion with Jesus Christ is life indeed! Knowing the inner reality by revelation and forms of prayer communion which emphasizes His internal dwelling or habitation. This is the inward journey.

B. The Mystical Arena of His Presence within Us
The mystical realm does not originate from the New Age movement or eastern mysticism. Satan has robbed the body of Christ of biblical truth (Jn. 10:10). Let us take our ground back! We are to be a people of revelation (Eph. 1:17). We are to be a chosen prophetic generation. Col. 1:11 – Jesus Christ in us is the hope of Glory. Therefore we need to find Him who has taken up residence with in through the new creation realities.

C. Three Attitudes to Cultivate in Prayer

1. Passive or reflective forms of prayer
2. Responsive forms of prayer
3. Aggressive forms of prayer

A book I would recommend you all read would be *Prayer: Finding the Heart's True Home*, by Richard J. Foster

II. DEFINING DEFINITIONS

A. Contemplative Prayer – A Review

1. Contemplative means to gaze at intently, to think, to study, to expect, to muse, to mediate.
2. Muse: to think on, to consider deeply, the mediate.
3. Meditate: to plan, intent, to think deeply, reflect.
4. Reflect: to throw back light, heat or sound, to give back an image or mirror, to bring or come back as a consequence as reflected glory.
5. Reflect on: to contemplate, to ponder on, to cast blame or to discredit, to meditate, to be thoughtful.

B. Called by a Dream

I was given a dream: and it said, "I will reveal to the hidden streams of the prophetic." This deals with the teaching and truths of the desert fathers and Christian mystics of ages past. The Holy Spirit is calling forth a new "quietist movement where the truths of past will be restored to us."

C. Inner Fire Carriers

The Quakers, John of the Cross, Madame Guyon, William Law, Teresa of Avila, Andrew Murray and many others are such examples. These people were maintainers of the inner fire. Parabolically they were like bow and arrow hunters, that would sit in quiet until the Lord would paint a target and in His presence they would release the arrow. If you hunt with too much noise you will scare off the target - the deer that pants by the water brook.

Yes, this is a road less traveled. Yet as you venture out into this quiet stream, you will find it is familiar territory just in a different language, called communion with God.

D. Scriptures to Ponder

1. Ps. 46:10 – *Be still, and know that I am God; I will be exalted among the nations, I will be exalted in the earth.* NIV
2. Heb. 12:2 – *Let us fix our eyes on Jesus, the author and perfecter of our faith, Who for the joy set before Him endured the cross, scorning its shame, and sat down at the right hand of the throne of God.* NIV
3. Eph. 1:17-19 – *I keep asking that the God of our Lord Jesus Christ, the glorious Father, may give you the Spirit of wisdom and revelation, so that you may know Him better. I pray also that the eyes of your heart may be enlightened in order that you may know the hope to which He has called you, the riches of His glorious*

inheritance in the saints, and His incomparably great power for us who believe. That power is like the working of His mighty strength.

4. Heb. 4:14-16 – *Therefore, since we have a great high priest who has gone through the heavens, Jesus the Son of God, let us hold firmly to the faith we profess. For we do not have a high priest who is unable to sympathize with our weaknesses, but we have one Who has been tempted in every way, just as we are - yet was without sin. Let us then approach the throne of grace with confidence, so that we may receive mercy and find grace to help us in our time of need.* NIV

III. WE ARE THE TEMPLE OF THE LIVING GOD

A. Scriptures

Slowly read the following two verses. Pause. Let the revelation of them sink into your being.

1. Cor. 3:16 – *Don't you know that you yourselves are God's temple and that God's Spirit lives in you?* NIV
2. Cor. 6:17 – *But he who unites himself with the Lord is one with Him in spirit.* NIV
3. Cor. 6:19 – *Do you not know that your body is a temple of the Holy Spirit, who is in you, whom you have received from God? You are not your own.* NIV

B. Moses' Tabernacle – A Shadow of Things to Come

Moses' Tent of Dwelling was divided into three sections.

1. Outer Court
2. Inner Court
3. Most Holy Place beyond the veil (Heb. 9:1-15).

C. Inside the Most Holy Place

1. Ark of the Covenant – contained within the Ark were three objects.
    a) Tablets of the Ten Commandments (the word of God).
    b) The Manna from the wilderness (the bread of life – Jn. 6).
    c) Aaron's rod that budded (the authority of God)
2. Above and around the Ark
    a) Covering cherubs were on each end of the top of the Ark in posture of worship.
    b) Between the cherubs was the Mercy Seat of the Lord.

c)   The smoke of His presence would come after the priest would minister before the Lord and take the coals from off the fire mingle it with the incense (prayer of the saints).

d)   The glory of the Lord would form and God would commune with them there.

D.   Progressive Pattern

There is a progressive pattern of the priest in approaching the Lord's presence. We must learn these ways of God in each generation.

1.   Washed in the blood of the Lamb – The Altar of Sacrifice.
2.   Washed in the water of God's Word – The Laver – Eph. 5:26.
3.   Lit up with the seven spirits. The seven lamps of the Candlestick.
4.   Fellowship at the body of Christ, the 12 tribes of Israel, the many members of the Lord's body – Table of Showbread.
5.   Altar of fire – incense and the mingling of incense – Ps. 144 This fifth station of grace was between the Holy and Most Holy Place. It was positioned right in front of the curtain that separated the two sections. It was a symbol of how we go from prayer to His presence.

E.   A Living Reality – Points to Remember

1.   We are God's temple, the Ark of His dwelling. The Word of God dwells in us richly.
2.   As a believer I am the dwelling place of God; a carrier of His presence. I become a priest that carries His presence.
3.   There is a processional journey into His presence. You must learn to shut off the worldly distractions to enter in.
4.   In this type of communal prayer, you must come into a quiet room. In Contemplative Prayer you pull down the shades, shut the doors behind you, removing yourself from worldly desires and come into the inward place.
5.   Your mind at this stage can be flooded with the many "lists of things to do". To deal with it, these thoughts:
     a)   Write them down.
     b)   Don't pay attention to them – These thoughts are vying for your attention or are like a lure of evil to draw you away.
     c)   The noise of pain often speaks. This realm of reflective mediation heals you as it is a form of transforming prayer. You now soak in the presence of God Almighty.
6.   The Holy Place can be a place of gifts and revelation and though they can be wonderful, they may become a place of distractions to you from going deeper in intimacy with Christ.

7. You can proceed further into the Most Holy Place. This was a place where there was no natural light, a place of apparent darkness, a room of silence, where there is nothing else but God alone. The Quakers called it 'the center of quiet' or 'centering'.

IV. REMINDING GOD OF HIS WORD

A. Primary Verse
Isaiah 62:6-7 – *On your walls, O Jerusalem, I have appointed watchmen; all day and all night they will never keep silent. You, who remind the Lord, take no rest for yourselves; and give Him no rest until He establishes and makes Jerusalem a praise in the earth.*

B. Of What Do We Remind Him?
Wesley Duewel in his book *Mighty Prevailing Prayer* presents to us seven things we are to remind God of.

1. Plead the honor and glory of God's name
2. Plead God's relationship to you
3. Plead God's attributes
4. Plead the sorrows and needs of the people
5. Plead the past answers to prayer
6. Plead the word and the promises of God
7. Plead the blood of Jesus

For more on this subject see notes on 'Pleading Our Case: Biblical Basis for Pleading Our Argumentation before God' in the study guide entitled *Watchmen on the Walls*.

C. A Prerequisite
In order to remind God of His Word, we must first be intimately acquainted with this precious book of promises, the Bible. Let us review the writings of Andrew Murray from his great book *With Christ in the School of Prayer*.[1]

If ye abide in Me, and My words abide in you, ye shall ask what ye will, and it shall be done unto you. (Jn. 15:7, KJV)

The vital connection between the Word and prayer is one of the simplest and earliest lessons of the Christian life. As the newly converted heathen put it, "I pray – I speak to my Father; I read – my Father speaks to me." Before prayer, God's Word strengthens me by giving my faith its justification and petition. In prayer, God's Word prepares me by revealing what the Father wants me to ask. After prayer, God's Word brings me the answer, for in it the Spirit allows me to hear the Father's voice.

It is the connection between His Word and our prayer that Jesus points to when He says, *"If ye abide in Me, and My words abide in you, ye shall ask what ye will, and it shall be done unto you"*. The deep importance of this truth becomes clear if we notice the expression, which this one replaces. More than once Jesus said, *"Abide in Me and I in you"*. His abiding in us was the complement and the crown of our abiding in Him. But here, instead of Ye in Me and I in you, He says, Ye in Me and My words in you. The abiding of His words is the equivalent of Himself abiding.

God is the infinite Being in whom everything is life, power, spirit, and truth - in the very deepest meaning of the words. When God reveals Himself in His words, He does indeed give Himself - His love and His life, His will and His power – to those who receive these words, in a reality that surpasses our comprehension. In every promise, He gives us the power to grasp and possess Himself. In every command, He allows us to share His will, His holiness, and His perfection. God's Word gives us God Himself!

That Word is nothing less than the Eternal Son, Christ Jesus. Therefore, all of Christ's words are God's words, full of a Divine and quickening life and power. *The words I speak unto you, they are spirit and they are life. ...if My words abide in you.* The condition is simple and clear. In His words, His will is revealed. As the words abide in me, His will rules me. My will becomes the empty vessel which His will fills, and the willing instrument which His will rules.

(For more on this subject see the study guide *Strategies of Intercession* in the lesson – "Reminding God of His Word.")

V.   BRINGING IT ALL TOGETHER

A.   Discovering Your Prayer Anointing

1.   There are many distinct or specialty graces or anointings in prayer. Some of these are praying a list, Israel prayer, prayer walking, praying for those in authority, missionary prayer, revival prayer, crisis intercession, etc.

2.   As we have seen in previous lessons and in other complimentary study guides, we each have a special grace gift. Let us each discover our position and cultivate it with faithfulness.

B. Contemplative Prayer + Scriptural Praying = Prophetic Intercession

When you wed or unite quiet communal prayer with reminding God of His Word, revelatory prayer or prophetic intercession will be born.

1. In prophetic intercession you shed your thoughts and opinions and agree and ask in His name. In this, you touch Him and He touches you.

2. In prophetic intercession we pick up the revelatory heart of God about a matter and in utter dependency pray it back to the Father, birthing the promise into being. In this, we are nothing more than a clay vessel of which He flows through as we kneel on His promises. For more on this tremendous subject refer to my book, The *Prophetic Intercessor*. Also my study guide called *Compassionate Prophetic Intercession*.

3. Prophetic intercession asks not merely that men might make decisions for Christ. It assumes the larger boundary of the great purposes of God. We plead for maturity of Christ in those who respond – that the new society of the redeemed mankind may expand unto the ends of the earth.

4. Whether it is preached truth, prayed burden, or spontaneous utterance, a thing is only prophetic if it brings a generation into knowledge of the heart of God for our time!

C. Two Summary Definitions

1. Prophetic intercession is the ability to receive an immediate prayer request from God and pray about it in a divinely anointed utterance.

2. Prophetic intercession is waiting before God in order to "hear" or receive God's burden (God's Word, His concern, warning, conditions, vision, or promises), responding back to the Lord and then to the people with appropriate actions.

D. Pleads the Promise

1. Prophetic intercession paves the way for the fulfillment of the prophetic promise.

2. In prophetic intercession, the Spirit of God pleads the covenant promises of God made to His people throughout history. Every unfulfilled promise ever made is to be pleaded by the Spirit before the throne.

3. Prophetic intercession is an urging to pray, given by the Holy Spirit, for situations or circumstances about which you have very little knowledge in the natural. You pray for the prayer requests that are on the heart of God. He nudges you to pray so that He

can intervene. God will direct you to pray to bring forth His will on the earth as it is willed in heaven.

4. It is not the promoting of a form, but the promoting of Him. We look and gaze upon His eyes of love, which are gazing back at us. Love, revelation, intimacy and communion proceed forth.

E. Application

Ask the Holy Spirit to lay His hand on you and give you a promise that you are to remind Him of. (Isa. 58, Ps 24, 37, Josh. 24:24, Lk. 4:18, Joel 2, Acts 2:38, Acts 10:38, Rom. 11:1).

Now pray it back to the Father as the Holy Spirit burdens you with that scripture.

VI. THE WAY IN IS NOW THE WAY BACK OUT

Realize this; once the priest made his progressive approach to the presence of God, though I am sure he wanted to, he did not remain forever in the Most Holy Place. He would then turn and pass back through the veil, past the altar of incense, the table of showbread, the golden candlestick, the laver, and the altar of sacrifice. Then he would pass out from the outer court to where the people lived.

Such is true in our lives. We must learn this path of walking though the tabernacle into the amazing place of His glorious presence. But then we must now carry His presence out to a world that is waiting. But be encouraged that you will not go out as the same person who entered.

You have been changed! You have picked up the secret of life. Now transmit His radiant glory wherever you go.

Also realize this, once you have learned this path less taken, it will be easier each time to pass through the noise of many voices, to quiet your soul before the Lord and commune with Him. Why? Because you have tasted the goodness of the Lord and can't wait to go back in.

Yes, the "Inward" is for the "Outward." Mary and Martha can kiss one another and you can learn the consecrated path of contemplative prayer by looking at the Old Testament shadow of "Walking through the Tabernacle" and like the priest of old, pick up the fragrance of the smoke of your garments and now carry it (Him) to a world aching to see, touch, and know a God who loves them.

Reflection Questions
Lesson Twelve: Walking through the Tabernacle

Answers to these questions can be found in the back of the study guide.

1. In order to remind God of His Word, we must first be acquainted with this precious book of promises, the Bible. Ask the Holy Spirit to lay His hand on you and give you a promise that you are to remind Him of from the scriptures. Such examples may be Isa. 58; Ps 24, 37; Josh. 24:24; Lk. 4:18; Joel 2; Acts 2:38, 10:38; Rom. 11:1 etc. Now pray that back to the Father as the Holy Spirit burdens you with a scripture. Write down your experience.

2. Position yourself before the Lord in entering His presence, to ask for the revelatory heart of God about a matter and in utter dependency pray it back to the Father, until the promise is birthed into being. (Remember in prophetic intercession you shed your thoughts and opinions and agree and ask in His name.)

3. We must learn this path of "walking though the tabernacle" into the amazing place of His glorious presence. But then we must now carry His presence out to a world that is waiting. Like the priest of old, pick up the fragrance of the smoke of your garments and now carry it (Him) to a world aching to see, touch and know that God loves them. Ask the Lord for specific application to this question as you seek to touch this lost world.

Answers to Reflection Questions

Lesson One: The Inward for the Outward
1. Quietness, Confidence
2. Law, Aaron's rod, Pot of manna
3. Father, Me (Jesus), In
4. Temple
5. Presence
6.   True   7. True   8. True

Lesson Two: What True Communion Requires – Part One
1. Cease striving, fret not, let go, relax
2. Union
3. TV Phone, Elevated thoughts, Books to read, People
4. Weapon
5. Secrets
6.   True   7. True   8. False

Lesson Three: What True Communion Requires – Part Two
1. Guard post, Keep watch
2. Secluded place, praying
3. Confession, forgiveness, removing, forgetting
4. Room
5. Weapons
6.   False   7. True   8. True

Lesson Four: Listening Waiting and Watching In Prayer
1. Listening, watching, waiting
2. Tent, Meeting
3. Lack of faith, commitment, or teaching, Fear of deception or error, Sin, Unbelief
4. Watchman
5. Waits
6.   False   7. True   8. True

Lesson Five: Contemplative Prayer – What It Is Not
1. Beholding, Transformed
2. Striving, Know
3. Jesus, Cross
4. Me
5. service
6.   True   7. True   8. True

Lessons Six to Twelve will include your own answers as you ponder these questions.

Resource Materials

Elizabeth Alves, *The Mighty Warrior*, Bulverde: Intercessors International, 1987.

Helen Bacovcin, Translator, *The Way of a Pilgrim* and *The Pilgrim Continues His Way*: Spiritual Classics from Russia, New York, NY: Image Books Doubleday, 1992.

Mike Bickle – Charisma, 2000.

Mike Bickle, "A Personal Prayer List", Kansas City, MO: MCF, 1988.

Mike Bickle, *Oasis: Dynamic Intercession*, Milton Keynes: Frontier Publishing International, Ltd., 1993.

Paul E. Billheimer, *Destined for the Throne*, Minneapolis, MN: Bethany House Publishers, 1975.

Henry T. Blackaby and Claude V. King, *Experiencing God*, Nashville TN, Broadman Press, 1994.

Dietrich Bonhoeffer, *The Way to Freedom,* Harper & Row, 1966.

E. M. Bounds, *The Complete Works of E. M. Bounds on Prayer*, Grand Rapids, MI: Baker Book House, 1990.

Paul F. Bradshaw, *Two Ways of Praying*, Abingdon Press, Nashville, TN: 1995.

Brother Lawrence and Frank Laubach, *Practicing His Presence*, Auburn, MA: Christian Books, 1973.

Ralph Carmichael, Lexicon/Light Records.

Guy Chevreau, *Pray with Fire: Interceding in the Spirit*, Toronto, ONT, Canada: Harper Perennial – Harper Collins Publishers Ltd., 1995.

Germaine Copeland, *A Call to Prayer: Intercession in Action*, Tulsa, OK: Harrison House, 1991.

Terry Crist, *Interceding Against the Power of Darkness*, Tulsa, OK: Terry Crist Ministries, 1990.

Joy Dawson, *Intimate Friendship with God*, Old Tappen, NJ: Chosen Books, Fleming H. Revell Co., 1986.

Wesley L. Duewel, *Mighty Prevailing Prayer*, Grand Rapids, MI: Francis Asbury Press, 1990.

Wesley L. Duewel, *Touch the World through Prayer*, Grand Rapids, MI: Zondervan Publication, 1986.

Dick Eastman, *Change the World School of Prayer*, Studio City, CA: World Literature Crusade, 1976.

Dick Eastman, *No Easy Road: Inspirational Thoughts on Prayer*, Grand Rapids, MI: Baker Book House, 1971.

Dick Eastman, *The Hour that Changes the World: A Practical Plan for Personal Prayer*, Grand Rapids, MI: Baker Book House, 1978.

Francois de Fenelon, *The Seeking Heart*, Beaumont, TX: The Library of Spiritual Classics, The SeedSowers, 1992.

P. T. Forsyth, D.D., *The Soul of Prayer*, Salem: Schmul Publishing Co., Inc., 1986.

Richard J. Foster, *Prayer: Finding the Heart's True Home*, New York, NY: Harper San Francisco, A Division of Harper Collins Publishers, 1992.

Richard J. Foster, *Prayers from the Heart*, New York, NY. Harper San Francisco, Harper Collins Publishers, 1994.

Richard J. Foster and James Bryan Smith, *Devotional Classics: Selected Readings for Individuals & Groups*, New York, NY: Harper San Francisco, A Division of HarperCollins Publishers, 1993.

Francis Frangipane, *The House of the Lord*, Lake Mary: Creation House, 1991.

Gordon P. Gardiner, *Radiant Glory: The Life of Martha Wing Robinson*, Brooklyn, NY: Bread of Life, 1962.

Pat Gastineau, *Contemplative Prayer*, Word of Love Ministries, Roswell GA.

Jean Nicholas Grou, *How to Pray*, London, Thomas Baker, 1901.

Norman Grubb, *Rees Howells Intercessor*, Fort Washington: Christian Literature Crusade, 1987.

Jeanne Guyon, *Experiencing God through Prayer*, Donna C. Arthur, Editor, Springdale, PA: Whitaker House, 1984.

Kenneth E. Hagin, *The Art of Intercession: Handbook on How to Intercede*, Tulsa, OK: Kenneth Hagin Ministries, 1987.

Steve Hawthorne and Graham Kendrick, *Prayer-walking: Praying On Site with Insight*, Lake Mary: Creation House, 1993.

Jack W. Hayford, *Prayer is Invading the Impossible*, Gwent: Bridge Publishing (U.K.), 1985.

Intercessors for America, *USA Pray! Training Manual*, Reston, VA: Intercessors for America, 1989.

Mary Alice Isleib, *Effective Fervant Prayer*, Minneapolis, MN: Mary Alice Isleib Ministries, 1991.

Cindy Jacobs, *Possessing the Gates of the Enemy*, Tarrytown: Fleming H. Revell Company, 1991.

Wayne Jacobsen, *A Passion for God's Presence*, Eugene, OR: Harvest House Publishers, 1991.

Rick Joyner, *The World Aflame: The Welsh Revival And Its Lessons For Our Time*, Charlotte, NC: MorningStar Publications 1993.

Thomas Keating, *Open Mind, Open Heart*, New York, NY: The Continuum Publishing Co., 1986.

Morton T. Kelsey, *Companions on the Inner Way: The Art of Spiritual Guidance*, New York, NY: The Crossroad Publishing Co., 1983.

Gordon Lindsay, *Prayer and Fasting: The Master Key to the Impossible*, Dallas, TX: Christ for the Nations, Inc. 1979.

Martyn Lloyd-Jones, *Enjoying the Presence of God*, Ann Arbor, MI: Servant Publications, 1991.

Adapted from the Teachings of Dr. Steve Meeks, Calvary Community Church, Houston, TX.

Don Milan Jr., *The Lost Passions of Jesus*. Copyright 1999; Mercy Place, Destiny Image, Publishers, Inc.; P.O. Box 310, Shippensburg, Pa. 17257-0310.

Andrew Murray, *Abide in Christ*, Copyright 1979 by Whitaker House. Whitaker House 580 Pittsburgh St. Springdale, Pa. 15144.

Andrew Murray, *Absolute Surrender*, Springdale, PA: Whitaker House, 1982.

Andrew Murray, *Like Christ*, Springdale, PA: Whitaker House, 1981.

Andrew Murray, *Waiting on God*, Springdale, PA: Whitaker House, 1981.

Andrew Murray, *With Christ in the School of Prayer*, Springdale, PA: Whitaker House, 1981.

Don Nori, *Secrets of the Most Holy Place*, Shippensburg, PA: Destiny Image, 1992.

Henri J. M. Nouwen, *The Way of the Heart*, New York, NY: Ballantine Books, 1983.

Henri J. M. Nouwen, *Making All Things New*, New York, NY: Ballantine Books, 1983.

Ben Patterson, *Waiting: Finding Hope When God Seems Silent*, Downers Grove, IL, InterVarsity Press, 1989.

Derek Prince, *Blessing or Curse: You Can Choose!*, Old Tappan, NJ: Chosen Books, 1990.

Derek Prince, *Fasting*, Fort Lauderdale, FL: Derek Prince Ministries, 1986.

Derek Prince, *How to Fast Successfully*, Fort Lauderdale, FL: Derek Prince Ministries, 1976.

Derek and Ruth Prince, *Prayers and Proclamations*, Fort Lauderdale, FL: Derek Prince Ministries - International, 1990.

Derek Prince, *Praying for the Government*, Fort Lauderdale, FL: Derek Prince Publications, 1970.

Derek Prince, *Shaping History through Prayer and Fasting*, Fort Lauderdale, FL: Derek Prince Ministries, 1973.

Leonard Ravenhill, *A Treasury of Prayer: The Best of E. M. Bounds on Prayer in a Single Volume*, Minneapolis, MN: Bethany House Publishers, 1981.

Leonard Ravenhill, *Revival Praying*, Minneapolis, MN: Bethany House Publishers, 1962.

Leonard Ravenhill, *Why Revival Tarries*, Minneapolis, MN: Bethany House Publishers, 1959.

Tricia McCary Rhodes, *The Soul at Rest*, Bethany House Publishers Minneapolis, MN, 1996.

David Runcorn, *A Center of Quiet: Hearing God When Life is Noisy*, Downers Grove, IL: InterVarsity Press, 1990.

Gwen Shaw, *Redeeming the Land*, Jasper: Engeltal Press, 1987.

Dutch Sheets, *Intercessory Prayer – The Lightning of God*, Dallas, TX: 1986.

Ed Silvoso, *That None Should Perish: How to Reach Entire Cities for Christ through Prayer Evangelism*, Ventura, CA: Regal Books, 1994.

A. B. Simpson, *The Life of Prayer*, Camp Hill: Christian Publications, 1989.

Kjell Sjoberg, *Winning the Prayer War*, Chichester: New Wine Press, 1991.

Bob Sorge, *In His Face*, Canandaigua, NY: Oasis House, 1994.

Sam Storms, *Devotional Life Class Notes*, Grace Training Center, Kansas City.

Mary Ruth Swope, *Listening Prayer*, Springdale, PA: Whitaker House, 1987.

Dr. Siang-Yang Tan and Dr. Douglas H. Gregg, *Disciplines of the Holy Spirit: How to Connect to the Spirit's Power and Presence*, Zondervan Publishing House.

St. Teresa of Avila, *Interior Castle*, Translated and Edited by E. Allison Peers, New York, NY: An Image Book, Published by Doubleday, A Division of Bantam Doubleday Dell Publishing Group, Inc., 1989.

Peter Toon, *Meditating as a Christian*, Harper Collins.

Elmer L. Towns, *Biblical Meditation for Spiritual Breakthrough*, Regal Books.

Elmer L. Towns, *Fasting for Spiritual Breakthrough*, Ventura, Ca. Regal Books 1996, pp. 20-23.

Mark and Patti Virkler, *Communion with God*, Shippensburg, PA: Destiny Image, 1990.

Mark and Patti Virkler, *Counseled by God*, Woy Woy, Australia: Peacemakers Ministries Ltd., 1986.

C. Peter Wagner, *Engaging the Enemy: How to Fight and Defeat Territorial Spirits*, Ventura, CA: Regal Books, 1991.

C. Peter Wagner, *Warfare Prayer*, Ventura, CA: Regal Books, 1992.

Arthur Wallis, *God's Chosen Fast*, Fort Washington: Christian Literature Crusade, 1968.

Donald S. Whitney, *Spiritual Disciplines for the Christian Life,* NavPress, 1991.

Dallas Williard, *The Spirit of the Disciplines: Understanding How God Changes Lives*, New York, NY: Harper San Francisco, A Division of HarperCollins Publishers, 1991.

B. J. Willhite, *Why Pray?* Lake Mary: Creation House, 1988.

John Wimber, *Teach Us to Pray*, Anaheim, CA: Vineyard Ministries International.

.

End Notes

[1] Gordon P. Gardiner, *Radiant Glory: The Life of Martha Wing Robinson*, Brooklyn, NY: Bread of Life, 1962..

[2] Mark and Patti Virkler, *Communion with God,* Shippensburg, PA: Destiny Image, 1990.

[3] Jeanne Guyon, *Experiencing God through Prayer,* Donna C. Arthur, Editor, Springdale, PA: Whitaker House, 1984.

[4] Henri J. M. Nowven, *Making All Things New,* New York, NY: Ballatine Books, 1983.

[5] Jean Nicholas Grou, *How to Pray*, London, Thomas Baker, 1901.

[6] Andrew Murray, *Waiting on God*, Springdale, PA: Whitaker House, 1981.

[7] Op. cit., Virkler.

[8] Dallas Williard, *The Spirit of the Disciplines*: *Understanding How God Changes Lives*, New York, NY: Harper San Francisco, A Division of Harper Collins Publishers, 1991.

[9] Mary Ruth Swope, *Listening Prayer*, Springdale, PA: Whitaker House, 1987.

[10] Op. cit., Murray, pp. 87-90.

[11] Adapted from the Teachings of Dr. Steve Meeks, Calvary Community Church, Houston, TX.

[12] Op. cit., Virkler.

[13] Richard J. Foster, *Prayer: Finding the Heart's True Home*, New York, NY: Harper San Francisco, A Division of Harper Collins Publishers, 1992.

[14] Adapted from the Teachings of Dr. Steve Meeks, Calvary Community Church, Houston, TX.

[15] Op. cit., Foster.

[16] Op. cit., Williard.

[17] David Runcorn, *A Center of Quiet: Hearing God When Life is Noisy*, Downers Grove, IL: InterVarsity Press, 1990.

[18] Francois de Fenelon, *The Seeking Heart*, Beaumont, TX: The Library of Spiritual Classics, The SeedSowers, 1992.

[19] Op. cit., Williard.

[20] Op. cit., Runcorn.

[21] Op. cit. Richard J. Foster.

[22] *Devotional Classics: Selected Readings For Individuals & Groups*, Edited by Richard J. Foster and James Bryan Smith, New York, NY: Harper San Francisco, A Division of Harper Collins Publishers, 1993.

[23] Richard J. Foster, *Prayers from the Heart*, New York, NY: Harper San Francisco, Harper Collins Publishers, 1994.

[24] Ralph Carmichael, Lexicon/Light Records.

[25] St. Teresa of Avila, *Interior Castle*, Interior Castle, Translated and Edited by E. Allison Peers, New York, NY: An Image Book, Published by Doubleday, A Division of Bantam Doubleday Dell Publishing Group, Inc., 1989.

[26] Elmer L. Towns, *Biblical Meditation for Spiritual Breakthrough*, Regal Books, p. 21.

27   Op cit., Foster, *Prayer Finding the Heart's True Home,* p. 146.

28   Peter Toon, *Meditating as a Christian: Waiting upon God,* Harper Collins.

29   Dietrich Bonhoeffer, *The Way to Freedom,* Harper & Row, 1966.

30   Sam Storms, *Devotional Life Class Notes* (7 Guides to Meditating), Grace Training Center, Kansas City, MO.

31   Tricia McCary Rhodes, *The Soul at Rest,* Bethany House Publishers, Minneapolis MN: 1996.

32   Dr. Siang-Yang Tan and Dr. Douglas H. Gregg, *Disciplines of the Holy Spirit: How to Connect to the Spirit's Power and Presence,* Zondervan Publishing House.

33   Pat Gastineau, *Contemplative Prayer,* Copyright 1999, Word of Love Publications; Box. 216, Roswell, Georgia, 30077-0216..

34   Op. cit., Foster, *Prayer: Finding the Heart's True Home.*

35   Donald S. Whitney, *Spiritual Disciplines for the Christian Life,* NavPress, 1991.

36   Op cit., Dr. Siang-Yang Tan and Dr. Douglas H. Gregg.

37   Op. cit., Elmer L. Towns.

38   Op. cit., Storms.

39   Op. cit., Toon.

40   Op. cit., Toon.

41   Op cit., Towns, *Biblical Meditation for Spiritual Breakthrough.*

42   Tricia McCary Rhodes, *The Soul at Rest,* Bethany House Publishers, Minneapolis MN: p. 41.

43   Elmer L. Towns, *Fasting for Spiritual Breakthrough,* Ventura, CA: Regal Books 1996, pp. 20-23.

44   Ibid., Elmer L. Towns, pp. 228-231.

45   Mike Bickle – Charisma, 2000.

46   Arthur Wallis, *God's Chosen Fast,* Fort Washington, Pennsylvania: Christian Literature Crusade, 1977, pp. 25-26.

47   Henry T. Blackaby and Claude V. King, *Experiencing God,* Nashville TN: Broadman Press, 1994.

48   Andrew Murray, *Abide in Christ,* Copyright 1979, Springdale, PA: Whitaker House.

49   Op. cit., Fenelon.

50   Op. cit., Runcorn.

51   Brother Lawrence – *The Practice of the Presence of God.* Copyright 1982 by Whitaker House, 580 Pittsburgh St., Springdale, Pa 15144.

52   Ibid., Brother Lawrence.

53   From the writings of John Flavel – from Don Milan Jr.'s book, *The Lost Passions of Jesus.* Copyright 1999; Mercy Place, Destiny Image, Publishers, Inc.; P.O. Box 310, Shippensburg, Pa. 17257-0310.

54   Op. cit., Richard J. Foster. *Prayer: Finding the Heart's True Home.*

55   Op. cit., Gastineau.

56   Op. cit., Tricia McCary Rhodes, *A Soul at Rest.*

Resources

Encounters Network ~ changing lives ❖ impacting nations
P.O. Box 1653, Franklin, TN 37065
www.encountersnetwork.com | 1-877-200-1604

Encounters Network

Network Sponsorship

We need a host of people and churches who will arise and say, "We believe in God's call on EN and we will back you financially!"

Sponsorship Levels:

Benefits:

Foundation Sponsor

Any amount given monthy or a one time gift of $250-$999 per year

20% off EN Conference registration
15% off EN Bookstore through website and call center
Reserved seating at EN Conferences
Quarterly EN Update Packet
One Time Free Gift

Executive Sponsor

$100-$499 per month or a one time gift of $1,000-$4,999 per year

Foundation Sponsor Benefits PLUS
50% off EN Conference registration
20% off EN Bookstore through website and call center

Presidential Sponsor

$500 or more per month or a one time gift of $5,000 or more per year

Executive Sponsor Benefits PLUS
2 Free EN Conference registrations, registration is required
25% off EN Bookstore through website and call center

For more information please call 1-877-200-1604 or visit our website at www.encountersnetwork.com

COMPASSION ACTS
love taking action

Love Taking Action

- **Mission Projects**
  sending resources and volunteers to help meet specific needs

- **Rice Shipments**
  shipping fortified rice to fight hunger around the world

- **Emergency Relief**
  responding to natural disasters through food and humanitarian aid

- **Project Dreamers Park**
  buidling playgrounds and community centers to inspire children to dream

- **First Nations in America**
  serving Native Americans by providing food, health supplies and education

Compassion Acts is a network of synergistic relationships between people, ministries and organizations, focused on bringing hope for our day through the power of compassion and prayer. We desire to demonstrate love and encourage the hearts of those impacted by poverty, disease, political strife and natural disasters through human relief efforts.

www.compassionacts.com

PRAYERSTORM

The Hour that Changes the World

Leviticus 6:13
"Fire must be kept burning on the altar continually; it must not got out."

Worldwide 24/7

Hourly Intercession Targeting:

- **Revival in the Church**
- **Prayer for Israel**
- **World's Greatest Youth Awakening**
- **Crisis Intervention through Intercession**

The vision of PrayerStorm is to restore and release the Moravian model of the watch of the Lord into churches, homes and prayer rooms around the world. Web-based teaching, prayer bulletins and resources are utilized to facilitate round-the-clock worship and prayer to win for the Lamb the rewards of His suffering.

Releasing the Global Moravian Lampstand

www.prayerstorm.com

Encounters Network
changing lives ❖ impacting nations

Changing Lives ❖ Impacting Nations

- **Empowering Believers**
  through training and resources

- **EN Media**
  relevant messages for our day

- **God Encounters Training**
  e-school of the heart

- **EN Alliance**
  a coalition of leaders

The vision of Encounters Network is to unite and mobilize the body of Christ by teaching and imparting the power of intercession and prophetic ministry, while cultivating God's heart for Israel. We accomplish this through networking with leaders in the church and marketplace; equipping believers through conferences and classes, utilizing various forms of relevant media; and creating quality materials to reproduce life in the Spirit.

www.encountersnetwork.com

Introduction to God Encounters Training School

If you are seeking to grow in your intimacy with God and mature in your walk of faith, if you desire to cultivate the spirit of revelation and live a life of power in the Spirit, then begin your journey by joining God Encounters Training – eSchool of the Heart.

Biblically-based study materials in both physical and electronic formats, combined with Spirit-led teaching, are now yours to experience on a personal level. These correspondence courses may be taken for credit towards graduation from the God Encounters Training School.

What Others Are Saying:

Goll's extraordinary ability to think through crucial issues and his skill at expressing the solutions in terms that the average believer can understand, comes through loud and clear in his materials.

~ **C. Peter Wagner**, noted author, professor, President of Global Harvest Ministries, Chancellor Emeritus of the Wagner Leadership Institute

The Lord has given James Goll insights into Scripture as it relates to the foundation of each believer and vision for the Body of Christ. His curriculum will powerfully strengthen the spiritual life of any person, group, or congregation that will use them.

~ **Don Finto**, author, pastor emeritus of Belmont Church in Nashville, TN and director of the Caleb Company

 For Course Information and Registration Visit
www.GETeSchool.com

GET eSchool Courses & Corresponding Study Guides

CHAMBER OF ACTION
EXPLORING PRINCIPLES - EXPERIENCING POWER

DELIVERANCE FROM DARKNESS

You shall know the truth and the truth shall set you free! Through this accessible and easy-to-use guide, you will learn how to: recognize demonic entities and their strategies, equip yourself to overcome the demonic, keep yourself refreshed during the fight, bring healing through blessing, and much more!

THE HEALING ANOINTING

In this thorough study guide, James W. Goll covers a range of topics including: The Healing Ministry of Jesus, How to Move In and Cooperate with the Anointing, Healing the Wounded Spirit, Overcoming Rejection, the Five Stage Healing Model, and much more.

RELEASING SPIRITUAL GIFTS

In this study guide, James draws from scripture and adds perspective from many diverse streams to bring you clear definitions and exhort you into activation and release. The topics covered are subjects like: How Does the Holy Spirit Move, What Offends the Holy Spirit, and many other lessons from years of experience.

REVIVAL BREAKTHROUGH

James W. Goll brings 12 solid teachings on topics like: Prophetic Prayers for Revival, Classic Characteristics of Revival, Fasting Releases God's Presence, Creating an Opening, Gatekeepers of His Presence, and much more. This manual will inspire you to believe for a breakthrough in your life, neighborhood, region, city and nation for Jesus' sake!

WAR IN THE HEAVENLIES

These carefully prepared 12 detailed lessons on spiritual warfare cover topics like: The Fall of Lucifer, Dealing with Territorial Spirits, The Weapons of Our Warfare, High Praises, The Blood Sprinkled Seven Times, and other great messages. This is one of James' most thorough and complete manuals.

CHAMBER OF LIFE
BUILDING OUR FOUNDATION - KNOWING TRUTHS, GROWING IN FAITH

A RADICAL FAITH

Whether you are a veteran spiritual warrior or new believer, this accessible, comprehensive guide lays out the enduring biblical fundamentals that establish the bedrock of belief for every mature Christian. This handbook will help you build an indestructible foundation of radical faith.

DISCOVERING THE NATURE OF GOD

These lessons focus on the knowledge of God Himself. Lessons include: Laying a Proper Foundation, The Authority of God's Word, The Effects of God's Word, God as Our Father, The Nature of God, The Attributes of God, Jesus the Messiah, and more. Learn the nature of God and thus be transformed into His image.

WALKING IN THE SUPERNATURAL LIFE

James W. Goll weds together a depth of the Word with a flow of the Spirit that will ground and challenge you to live in the fullness for which God has created you. Topics include The God Who Never Changes, Tools for the Tool Belt, Finishing Well, and much more.

TO PURCHASE THESE STUDY GUIDES INDIVIDUALLY & OTHER RELATED PRODUCT VISIT: WWW.ENCOUNTERSNETWORK.COM

For Course Information and Registration Visit
www.GETeSchool.com

GET eSchool Courses & Corresponding Study Guides

CHAMBER OF INTIMACY
BLUEPRINTS FOR PRAYER - PRELUDE TO REVIVAL

WATCHMEN ON THE WALLS

This original study guide is a classic in today's global prayer movement and covers many important and foundational lessons on intercession including: Fire on the Altar, Christ Our Priestly Model, The Watch of the Lord, From Prayer to His Presence, Identification in Intercession, and more.

COMPASSIONATE PROPHETIC INTERCESSION

These 12 lessons feature James W. Goll's finest teaching on the fundamentals of prophetic intercession and represent one of the primary messages of his life. Topics include Travail, Tears in the Bottle, Prophetic Intercession, The Power of Proclamation, Praying in the Spirit, and much more.

PRAYER STORM

This study guide sounds a worldwide call to consistent, persistent prayer for: revival in the church, the greatest youth awakening ever, Israel – and for all the descendents of Abraham, and God's intervention in times of major crises. Prayer Storm is an invitation into an international virtual house of prayer full of intercessors who commit to pray one hour per week.

PRAYERS OF THE NEW TESTAMENT

In this study guide, James goes through each of the scriptural prayers of the early church apostles and brings you a brief historical background sketch along with insights from the Holy Spirit for today. Learn what true apostolic intercession is, how to intercede with revelation, and how to cultivate a heart for your city and nation.

STRATEGIES OF INTERCESSION

In these 12 lessons, James W. Goll deals with issues like Confessing Generational Sins, Reminding God of His Word, Praying for Those in Authority, Praying on Site with Insight, and Praying Your Family into God's Family. It is a thorough and precise exposure to the many different strategies and models of prayer.

CONSECRATED CONTEMPLATIVE PRAYER

These 12 lessons have helped hundreds come into a deeper communion with their heavenly Father. James W. Goll brings understanding from the truths of Christian mystics of the past and builds on it with lessons from his own walk with the Lord. Topics include The Ministry of Fasting, Contemplative Prayer, Quieting Our Souls before God, and much more.

TO PURCHASE THESE STUDY GUIDES INDIVIDUALLY
& OTHER RELATED PRODUCT VISIT: WWW.ENCOUNTERSNETWORK.COM

For Course Information and Registration Visit
www.GETeSchool.com

Made in the USA
Charleston, SC
08 September 2012